Praise for *S*

"Sherry doesn't hold back as she tells her powerful story from the pain and shame of addiction to living freely and fully surrendered to Christ. She shares to empower others to also live in this freedom and grasp the healing and grace from our Lord Jesus Christ."

—Bonnie Gruppen, president,
Journey of Hope Yoga

"As I read this book I hear the honest, funny, raw, vulnerable, and brave voice of its author. Sherry has become her most authentic self through her journey to sobriety. This book takes you along for the ride, inspires you, and gives you hope for your own freedom."

—Carolyn Doyle, executive director,
Lakeshore Pregnancy Center, Holland, MI

SOBER CYCLE

PEDALING THROUGH RECOVERY
ONE DAY AT A TIME

SHERRY HOPPEN

NEW HOPE®
PUBLISHERS
Imprint of Iron Stream Media
Birmingham, Alabama

New Hope Publishers
100 Missionary Ridge
Birmingham, AL 35242
New Hope Publishers is an imprint of Iron Stream Media
NewHopePublishers.com
IronStreamMedia.com

Some names have been changed for privacy reasons. Iron Stream Media serves its authors as they express their views, which may not express the views of the publisher.

Library of Congress Control Number: 2021932253

ISBN-13: 978-1-56309-429-3
Ebook ISBN: 978-1-56309-430-9

1 2 3 4 5—25 24 23 22 21
Printed in the United States of America

Dedication

To my husband, who believed in me when I could not. Craig, your strength and love were there for me every single time I fell down and every single time I got back up. I am so blessed to have fallen in love with you twice in my life.

Thank you for going on this ride through life with me. I know that together, with God, we can do anything.

Except ride a tandem bike.

Love always,
Spark

Contents

My Gratitude List

I had no idea that writing this page for the book would be the most difficult. I simply didn't know where to start. There are so many people in my life who have spoken into my addiction and recovery—all contributors to my story that you are holding in your hands. Thank you. I cried the whole time I was writing this page.

Family

Craig: You have been my rock since the day God strategically positioned us to meet at the Hudsonville Fair almost forty years ago. I don't know where the last forty years went, but I do know this: I never wanted this to be my story—or write about it, for that matter. You told me once that without our story there wouldn't be this beauty on the other side of it. God is so good.

Abby, Loren, and Olivia: I am so grateful that God made you my kids. How do I say thank you for loving me through the process of addiction and recovery? I don't know how, but you did. I know it was confusing and hurtful at times, and I am thankful every day for the grace you have given me through it. My heart bursts with pride often at the adults you have become in this life. You make me so proud and I love you.

Joe, Stephanie, and Big Landon: While you were still a toddler, we were praying for you. We've been praying for our children's spouses since they were born. We knew God had that person already picked out, and we prayed you would grow in love for the Lord, and when the time was right he would introduce you to each other. And he did. Thank you for what you bring to this family. For being the one we prayed for and for loving each other through the beautiful days and the not so beautiful days. Nothing in life probably prepared you for Hoppenworld, but I think you are doing just fine. Love you all so much.

Landon: You made me Mimi for the first time, and nothing in this world could've have prepared me for what that would be like. You are the happy ending at the end of this book and the happy beginning of Mimi life for me. The first time I held you, I whispered in your ear, "Mimi's going to have to get you a bike." My happiest memory of last summer was going for ice cream on the bike together and sitting on that same bench outside the post office that I did when I was your age. I love you, little buddy.

Otto: I will always and forever be your Honey and love that you decided all by yourself to call me that. Never stop. You gave us quite a scare before you were even born and then for quite a while after, but it hasn't stopped you from being the amazing little boy that you are. I will never forget those first months of your life. You are a miracle to behold, and I thank God for your blond curls and healthy red cheeks every day. Honey loves you.

Levi: You call me Mimi, but not often. Unlike your Mimi, you are a little man of few words, but I get you. You will always be special to me. I can't look at you without seeing my little brother whose middle name is yours. Maybe not everyone sees it, but I have come to the conclusion that this is a gift from God and I gratefully accept it. Mimi loves you.

Thank you to *my parents* for teaching me to trust in the Lord my entire life and to my sweet mother-in-law, *Jan,* and our shared love of all things reading and raising her son to love and honor God too.

Friends

Amy VandeBunte, Angela LeRoux, Bonnie Gruppen, Carolyn Doyle, Dawn Glashower, Geri Allen, Lieza Bates, Robin Angott, Robin Vandenberg, Susan Boschma, and Tina Abdoo: You were all present at some point at my worst, and I hope by now you have seen my best. My biggest fear was losing my friends, and I was so wrong. What I have gained in my friendships is more than I could have ever imagined. Love you guys, and I put you in alphabetical order because you are all in first place in my heart.

Denise Frawley: You enlightened me about the committee. I had no idea what to call them! I love you, dancing queen.

Don Wickstra, Derek Owens, Jonna Lubbers, Amy Aeronauts, and the entire Ride4Life Team(s) and Lakeshore Pregnancy Center: You have all touched my life in more ways than you will ever realize.

Gary Feenstra: Thanks for dragging me to Maranatha. I am so grateful; its where I found myself back, and of course you found a job for me too. That's OK, I love the Maranatha Christian Writers Conference and the beginning it gave me. Thank you, my friend.

Rev. Dr. Tanner Smith: I needed all your godly wisdom. Just so you know, that's the only time I'll probably call you Dr., even though you've earned it. You'll always just be Tanner, the kid fresh off the grounds of Camp Geneva.

My Joyful Surrender ladies all over the US: You know who you are, and I am grateful every day you are a part of my world. We are so much more than recovery buddies. You are the connection I prayed for.

From the Book Process

Natalie Nyquist: You are the best editor and friend a newbie like myself could ask for. Thanks for not thinking I was a stalker when I asked you to get in my van.

Eddie Jones: Thanks for shaking your finger in my face and telling me, "People need to read your book." I started writing again the next day. Thank you.

Ramona Richards, Kim McCulla, Susan Cornell, and Tina Atchenson at Iron Stream Media: Thanks for your patience with a newbie, and to *Cyle Young* for getting it into their hands. Thank you for believing in me.

Most importantly I thank God, who tells us in Ephesians that he can "do immeasurably more than all we ask or imagine."
He wasn't kidding.

PART 1

SCARED

1

Unwelcome Invitation

September 2010

I had the worst hangover of my life. Instead of nursing it in the cocoon of my bed as usual, I was surrounded by family and friends and preparing to bike with nine other riders from Holland, Michigan, to Grapevine, Texas. Eleven hundred miles in eleven days. My bags were being loaded in a van, and the motor home going with us was being stocked with food and water. Ride4Life 2010 was almost ready to go. This was the real deal. I was in way over my head; there was no way out. I was going to be detoxing while riding a bike one hundred miles a day.

I was on this ride for all the wrong reasons—most of them selfish. I signed up to free myself from my destructive ways. Plus, I would surely lose weight in the process—the ultimate motivator for all women! But I didn't reap any of these benefits. Instead I was nursing a terrible hangover and hadn't lost an ounce since I had started training for this insane bike ride.

Why did I always find myself in these predicaments with no visible way out? Actually, there was a way out of this one: coming clean to everyone and admitting that I was an alcoholic coming off a three-day binge that ended earlier this morning. I was incredibly hungover, possibly still inebriated, and just needed to go home to bed. But there was no way I was going to confess that to anyone. I guarded my secret so closely that I

3

was choosing to suffer through one hundred miles a day on a bike rather than expose myself.

How did I get here? Why didn't I just go to a meeting like everyone else who drank too much? I always chose the hard way to do things. This time it was more to impress others than to heal myself—always an I'll-show-them way of thinking. Instead of following a more conventional path to sobriety, I signed up for a fundraising bike ride from Michigan to Texas. Surely there was an easier way! But when I remember who I was when I received the invitation to join this trip—an overweight, out-of-shape, nonathletic, supposedly drying-out alcoholic—there is no doubt it was a God thing. It certainly wasn't the method I would've chosen to get sober, but here I was.

Three months earlier

My husband, Craig, and son, Loren, were going on an Alaskan cruise—without me. We had won the trip through our business, but I would not be going for several reasons. For one, our youngest daughter was graduating from eighth grade, and her graduation was during the cruise. I hope she someday recalls that it was Mom who stayed back from an Alaskan cruise for her eighth-grade graduation.

I promised Craig that I wouldn't drink while he was gone, and I meant it. I don't know what made that time different. I wanted him to have a good time without worrying about what was happening at home. Craig had no reason to believe that I would keep my promise this time; I'd broken so many in the past.

Truth be told, I was grateful for a valid excuse not to go, even though I didn't voice that to my family. Based on past experience, I knew I could not handle a cruise where the drinks were free and flowed 24/7. We had been a part of this business group for most of my adult life, and many of the members knew I'd officially quit drinking; I was supposed to be sober. If I went on the cruise, I knew that I would drink, and it would be ten days of secrets, blackouts, and hiding games.

So my son went instead of me. Plus, the trip took place over his twenty-first birthday. I couldn't go along and celebrate a birthday that was all about drinking when I couldn't drink; my son could, and others would buy him shots, and I would watch and salivate! That party would have to go on without me.

They left. I battled depression. Why did I make that promise to Craig not to drink? I wasn't working, and I'd cut myself off from any social life. I just didn't know how to do life socially sober; it was easier to be alone.

I woke up each morning in darkness and stayed there. I spent the first three days getting my daughter off to school each morning and then doing absolutely nothing but attending my personal pity party. It was an easy party to get ready for. No shower or makeup. Yesterday's clothes. I just made myself presentable by the time my daughter Olivia came home from school.

Early one morning—about four days into this lame party I was hosting—my phone rang. The caller ID told me it was the Lakeshore Pregnancy Center (LPC), where I used to work, and for some reason I answered. I didn't do that very often— answer the phone. There really wasn't anyone that I wanted to talk to.

"Hi, Sherry. How are you?" It was the assistant director; I'd always liked her.

"Pretty good, thanks," I replied. "How are you?" It was good to hear her voice.

"Desperate! We are so short of volunteers today that I was wondering if there is any way you could come in? If you could answer phones, that would really help us out."

I hesitated for a moment and looked in the mirror from where I sat on the bottom of the staircase. The woman in the mirror looked pretty rough; maybe getting out of the house was a good idea. "OK," I said with as much enthusiasm as Eeyore, then went upstairs to take a shower and begin a day away from myself.

As I got ready, I realized that it felt good to have a purpose for the day instead of just wandering around the house thinking about all the things I should be doing. I couldn't help but think that this was good: a whole day would pass where I could be safe and not drink. I'd be one day closer to my husband returning—so I could drink again. Planning to drink after his return was the only thing keeping me sober while he was gone.

I answered phones and caught up with my former coworkers, many of whom were good friends (just not close enough to know my secrets). All day as I sat at that desk, I kept thinking that no one had any idea of the trouble I was in. I was filled with self-loathing—along with jealousy that no one else dealt with an addiction like mine.

I was sure that I was one of a kind. Who works in ministry, directs children's choir, is a team mom and respected member of the community, and drinks alone in her closet all day—and cannot stop? An addict. My shame level was at an all-time high. I was surrounded by people but felt completely alone.

At one point I took some messages upstairs to our executive director, Mark. He was a pastor in charge of a women's pregnancy center, and for that reason alone I respected him! When I handed him the messages, he looked right at me— or possibly through me—and said, "Where have you been hiding?"

Any strength to keep faking life left me as the mask I'd been hiding behind slid off. I sank down in the chair opposite his desk and hung my head. For once I couldn't hide what I didn't want anyone to see.

Get it together! I couldn't keep the tears from falling any more than I could stop the words spilling from my mouth, which made me feel frantic, exposed. *Why here? Why now?* My thoughts whirled as I tried to grasp what was happening.

"I was destroying everything in my path. Mostly my marriage and any other relationship with those closest to me." Notice I used the word *was* in this conversation. My guard was always up and even while confessing, I made sure that Mark would be led to think I was successfully conquering the battle of the bottle. "I've been sober for about five months"—*really only five days*—"and I am struggling to stay in recovery," I said with tears streaming down my cheeks.

Then—thank goodness—I regained control. "The only thing keeping me sober today is my promise to Craig that I would not drink while he is gone, so being here where it's 'safe' is a blessing." I thought this sounded very noble with just a touch of needy. A good place to end this conversation and make an exit. I'd said enough; I put my mask back on. My loss of control had been brief, and I was back to my alcoholic way of thinking. *What good can talking to someone do? He can't help me. Nobody can.*

The whole truth was too shameful to share. I was already fighting panic that my secret was no longer a secret at work. My reputation was already ruined at home; I couldn't lose it here!

Instead of feeling relief after unloading my struggles, I was mortified. Why was I so stupid as to let my guard down and expose my fears? I hadn't planned on spilling my guts. Now they were all laid out (well, most of them) for examination.

Mark took a minute before saying anything. *Just listen to what he has to say, nod your head, and say thank you.* He'd probably recommend scripture, or a meeting, maybe even a friend I should talk to who was going through the same thing. What he said next completely surprised me.

"You need to join us on the Ride4Life. We need more women."

2

Excuses

September 2010

"Fifteen minutes, riders!" Derek shouted. My head was pounding and my hands were shaking. I kept my fists tightly at my side so no one else would see the tremors. They would probably just think it was nerves, but I knew better.

I looked around at the other riders as they smiled and chatted with family and friends. Everyone seemed happy and relaxed, confirming my belief that the only one here with a hangover was me. When it came time to circle up and pray, I held my husband's hand tight, the tears were streaming down my face. There was no turning back. Why hadn't I stuck with the firm no I'd given Mark in his office? Instead, here I was getting ready to leave on a bike ride across the US.

I was here as a direct result of my husband's insistence and a firm nudge from God. I had been shocked when Mark's answer to my drinking woes was, "You need to join the Ride4Life." In that moment Mark's solution had seemed like an easy out: no advice or lecture—just the stupidest fix to my problem I'd ever heard. It was so unrealistic, not to mention laughable.

Mark had founded the Ride4Life with six other men the previous year. They went on a fundraising bike trip for the pregnancy center I was working at, riding from Holland, Michigan, to Baltimore, Maryland. When I say *bike*, I mean a pedal bike—not a motorcycle. They rode more than one hundred miles a day to reach Baltimore in a week.

During their trip I was working the front desk in the pregnancy center, and everyone kept asking if I'd heard from them, how were they doing, and weren't they amazing? In my head I was calling them Team Testosterone and thought it was the craziest thing I'd ever heard of. I couldn't fathom doing that day after day, nor did I have any desire to try.

So imagine my reaction when Mark said I should join this year's ride. Was he desperate for participants? I saw my escape from this awkward conversation. I laughed. "Thanks for your time, Mark, but no way." With that, I headed back to phone duty.

"Think about it," he called as I left.

On the way back to my desk, I stopped to see the director, my good friend Carolyn (the only one who knew about my struggle). I told her what Mark had said but didn't mention my confession. She smiled and said, "You should do it."

"Sure, join me," I said sarcastically as I walked away.

The day at work ended, and I was glad to realize that there were only five hours left before I could go to bed and escape life through sleep—just to get up and go through another whole day of fighting my cravings.

Thank goodness my daughter was going to be home tonight to help pass the long evening ahead.

෫෦෫෦෫෦

Later that night, I tried to read and found myself staring at the same lines over and over. Reading had always been my favorite pastime, but I hadn't been able to focus in a long time. Thanks for that, Vodka. Sitting there, lost in my thoughts with a book on my lap, I asked myself for the first time: *Could I do that bike trip?*

I allowed myself to fantasize for a few moments: how proud my family would be, how impressive it would look to my friends, and of course how fit my body would be as I rode across the finish line. After indulging in my daydreams for a few moments, I dismissed this unrealistic idea once again.

I went to bed grateful for another sober day, bringing me closer to the day I would drink again. That was the thought I went to sleep with every night. *I will drink again.*

I was looking forward to a great night's sleep, though. The longer I stayed sober, the better I slept. When I drank, I had no problem falling asleep (aka passing out). The problem was *staying* asleep. In the last few years I would wake up at around three a.m. full of anxious thoughts. *Why did I drink again? Did I black out? Does Craig know? Did I drink it all? Did I hide it well?*

I would usually get up and check my alcohol supply, and if there was any left I usually drank it and went right back to sleep. If I'd not planned well and there wasn't enough to get me through the night, I dealt with night sweats and paranoid thoughts until morning.

Tonight it would not be alcohol—or rather the lack of it—waking me up. In the middle of the night I was awakened out of deep sleep thinking, *Or can I? Can I what? That bike trip thing again? Where is this coming from?*

This was freaking me out. I knew it was the voice of God, and it scared me. I didn't want to do this. I needed my husband to come home and validate my thought process that this bike trip was unrealistic. I needed backup to tell God no.

By the time my husband came home, the stupid bike trip had been haunting me for six consecutive days and nights. I couldn't get it out of my head no matter how hard I tried! I didn't want to tell Craig, because what if he said that I should do it? I was sure that he would just assume it was another one of my big ideas to fix myself and tell me to go back to AA. *No thanks. I'm not setting myself up for that.* So I kept it to myself, and the nightly interruptions of my sleep continued.

A few days after Craig came home, we went out for dinner. He had been quiet since his return.

"Is something bothering you?" I asked.

He looked me in the eye. "I need to know if you drank while I was in Alaska."

"No, I didn't," I replied.

It felt really good to answer him honestly and see the look of relief on his face, knowing I kept from drinking while he was gone—and since he returned home. I told him about working at the center and how it helped pass the time. Then the dilemma I'd been struggling with came out like a diarrhea of the mouth.

"Oh, wait until you hear this. Mark asked me to do the Ride4Life. You know, that crazy, cross-country bike trip those guys did last year from here to Baltimore? Well, this year they're riding to Texas! I have no idea why he would even think to ask me! There is no way . . ."

As I rambled on, Craig put his hand up, trying to stop my torrent of words burying him. He looked me in the eyes and said, "I think you should do it."

My mouth dropped open. He was supposed to be my official way out of this! I had only one word for him. "Why?"

"Hon," he said as he took my hands in his across the table. "You told me you were a threefold mess. Physically, emotionally, and spiritually. That you wished that God would step in and take over, show you the way out of this."

Crap, he was right. I said I wanted a challenge that could truly change my life—but I couldn't imagine what that looked like. I went for a few walks while he was gone, read my Bible, and meditated. I was working on all three of those areas of my life—physical, emotional, and spiritual! Then—BAM—there it was: the reason that this bike ride wouldn't leave me alone. It addressed all three of those areas.

Physical: I would get in shape and let go of some unhealthy habits I'd acquired.

Emotional: It would be challenging and I would have to work hard to not let my addiction take over. Biking so much

11

would ensure that I didn't have a lot of spare time to indulge in drinking.

Spiritual: This could be the chance I'd been waiting for to get closer to God. I would have a lot of time to talk to God while I was riding. I'd been on my knees praying for a way out of alcohol's grip, and I knew God was telling me to get off my knees and on a bike. The message was loud and clear, but I still tried to deny that powerful voice.

I stared at Craig. "You think I should do it. Are you serious?"

"One hundred percent serious," he replied. "You're doing this. Go check out some bikes tomorrow, and you can show me what you've chosen after work."

I didn't argue. Maybe he would let it go after he thought about it more.

৪৩৩৪৩

Craig left for work the next morning after giving me a kiss on my cheek and a reminder to go to the bike store to get a feel for what I wanted. *How should I know what I want?* I kept my mouth shut and let him think that all was well and buying a bike was going to fix everything. "That's your assignment for today, young lady," he said sternly but with a smile.

After he left I decided to call my friend and coworker Derek, who had been part of the bike team the year before. *He'll be just the right person to talk to.* Being a friend, he would be totally honest with me and tell me that I was in no shape to do this. As humiliating as it would be, I was willing to set myself up for rejection just so someone would finally put an end to this madness. By the time Craig came home from work, I could tell him the invite to be a part of this ride had been rescinded.

Derek agreed to meet me. At least he was going to go easy on me and not shoot me down right away. I got ready to meet him on his lunch break. *What does one wear to a bike shop?* I stood in my closet. *Something sporty, I suppose.* I didn't have a whole lot of sporty clothes that I would wear anyplace other than the gym, so I decided on jeans and a T-shirt. Casual. Aloof.

When I got to the bike shop I didn't want to get out of my car. This was foreign territory—I'd never been in a bike shop. We were in the downtown shopping district. My stores were a little farther down the street, and I'd honestly never even noticed that there was a bike shop here! Derek was waiting, so I pasted a fake smile on my face and headed inside.

3

My New Friend the
Blue Bike

Derek totally let me down. He did not meet any of my expectations about ditching the whole bike thing. In fact, he was enthusiastic about the idea. I was far out of my remaining bits of comfort zone as we entered the bike shop and examined hardcore bikes. I learned that they were called road bikes, and they had the skinniest tires I'd ever seen.

I'd never owned anything except a Kmart ten-speed growing up and then a mom bike to pull the baby Burley while camping. These bikes were different: they had more bells and whistles than my car; they were meant for speed. Did I mention balance was key? Not one of my strong points. And how about those seats? They looked like some sort of torture for my rear! Did I mention the price? That alone should be enough to deter my husband from this crazy idea.

We didn't have a lot to choose from, so we quickly narrowed it down to a blue bike that I was assured would be perfect for me. I actually thought it was kind of ugly.

Speaking of ugly, I checked out the cycling apparel. Seriously? I don't think there is a sport with more unflattering apparel than this one. Well, maybe a wrestling singlet or a swimmer's Speedo, but cycling clothes were right up there with both of those. I knew exactly how I felt about skin-tight shorts with padding on the butt. Not to mention they cost seventy-five dollars. My favorite store down the street had a pair of shoes I had my eye on. I'd much rather spend the money on those.

I left the shop with the blue bike on hold, wishing I could have left a false name and number so that they could never again connect me to it. But with Derek next to me I was stuck and held accountable to decide on the bike within twenty-four hours.

Derek was so enthusiastic—totally not what I was expecting. "That one is for you!" he said.

"Thanks. I'll let you know what I decide."

Why did I say "I"? This decision had never been mine from the moment it came to my attention. It felt surreal, like I was the main character in a reality show.

Craig came home from work and, without even taking his coat off, said, "Did you pick out a bike?"

"Yes. I mean, I looked. But there wasn't a lot to choose from." I hoped he'd take the hint and we could drop this craziness about all things bike.

"Did you find anything?" he asked.

"Well, yeah, but I don't really like it."

"Why not?"

I tried to look as appalled as possible. "It's blue. I don't look good in blue. Red is more my color."

He stared at me for a long moment and shook his head. "Show me," he said.

Who is this guy? Out loud I said, "Whoa, buddy. Not only is it blue, it's super expensive—and that's for the stripped-down model. There are more gadgets to buy on top of that." At this point in the conversation, the financial angle was my best hope to deter him.

"Show me," he said again. So off we went to the bike shop. I recall thinking that I'd be a little sad when all this drama was over and I didn't have to think about it anymore. It kept me from thinking about alcohol—a lot! I'd still kept from drinking since Craig came home. I was planning on it as soon as this bike game was over. Maybe even tonight.

Well, it wasn't over yet. The clerk went over all the features with Craig while I tuned them out. I didn't care because we weren't buying one anyway. I was jolted back into reality when Craig said, "You should pick out a helmet."

In a trancelike state I did—and then gloves and a pair of ugly bike shorts. We left the shop—him pushing the bike to the truck and me trailing behind. "At least even if I don't do the trip, I might have a new hobby," I said.

He stopped, turned, and looked at me. "Oh, you are doing it."

I realized then that there was no turning back—we were both grasping at this bike trip to be a total game changer in our lives.

When we got home, Craig said, "It's still light out. Why don't you go for a spin?"

"I'm scared of riding on the road without practicing first."

Of course he had a simple solution. "Drive to the bike path. You can take my truck."

So I went inside and put on those wretched shorts. I felt like a sausage stuffed into fresh casing. I filled two water bottles like I was leaving for a fifty-mile ride and spent ten minutes in front of the mirror adjusting my helmet. Yes, I was procrastinating.

Craig opened the door and yelled, "Daylight's wasting! You better get going."

I wanted to flip him off—and I might have. . . . I went outside feeling utterly ridiculous, and he—of all things!—tried to take my picture. I quickly put an end to that idea.

The trail was only a few miles from our house, and as I stood in the parking lot at the trailhead, I smoked a cigarette. It was kind of ironic to stand there in full bike garb smoking a cigarette. Not exactly one of my finer athletic moments. I seriously debated smoking the entire time and just making it appear like I'd actually ridden.

Curiosity won out. "What would doing a few miles actually feel like?" I unloaded the bike and cautiously rode around the parking lot a few times. I worked up the courage to get on the path, and I was off! I quickly noted that my new fascination would definitely be my fancy odometer. It tracked my speed and distance. At the one mile mark I was elated! I'd just ridden a mile!

It wasn't that hard, so I kept going. I experimented with the gears and tried to get a feel for the bike. When I hit the five mile mark, I reluctantly turned around. I'd surprised myself; I actually wanted to keep going! However, if I didn't turn around I would run out of daylight.

When I pulled into the parking lot with ten miles on my odometer, I was impressed with myself. I kind of liked it. It was, for lack of a better word, freeing. For one hour I'd not thought about drinking or anything related to it. Instead, I actually accomplished something. That was amazing in itself. I wanted to go a little farther, but the sun had set, so it was time to load up the bike and call it a night.

When I got back I ran like a kid to my husband, shouting, "I did ten miles, I did ten miles!" I could tell he was proud of me, and he gave me a big hug.

In that moment, we had hope. A real hope that maybe things were going to get better this time. That night my sleep was interrupted a few times thinking about my new blue bike. *Today, I'm going to do fifteen miles!* I woke up excited to actually get on with my day for once.

Until I went out to the garage and eyeballed this foreign blue gadget leaning against the wall. No kickstand for road bikes, I was told. *What have I gotten myself into?*

The voice of doubt was creeping back in. I wasn't supposed to like riding. I stuffed myself into the dreaded shorts and decided to ride up and down the driveway a few times. That felt OK, but now what? We lived in the country, and I wanted to ride but I was too chicken to go out onto the road.

I had a fear bigger than falling off or getting hit by a car. Dogs—specifically dogs that chase cyclists. I'd grown up riding my bike in the country and had been chased by a dog or two back in the day. I am pretty sure I still have some PTSD from those chases because the thought of it happening again was enough for me to wheel the bike back into the garage and call it a day.

That night Craig approached me. "I see the bike moved. How far did you go?"

Great. Not only is he checking for hidden vodka bottles under my bathroom sink, he's marking where the dang bike is when he leaves in the morning.

"Around the driveway a few times," I answered defensively, wishing he would drop the whole bike thing.

"Really? It was gorgeous today. I thought you'd take a ride and see how it felt to go a little farther."

"Sorry to disappoint you," I said. "But I am freaked out about a few things—the two biggest being cars and dogs. I need to just ride it in the driveway for now." We did have a long driveway, but not *that* long. I'd basically ridden in circles a few times to add 0.33 miles to my odometer. Pretty sure that would not be considered a legitimate ride.

Craig looked a little exasperated. "Just take my truck and go to the trail."

Smart aleck. Of course you have all the answers. Why don't you go ride it and see how far you can go?

I thought it over for a second and formulated a plan. "Fine. I'll go after dinner."

I had a two-part plan. First, I would hang out at the trailhead until it was safe to come home. Second, I would stop at the liquor store on the way back. As the day progressed, I'd lost all my enthusiasm for riding and was starting to resent everything *bike*. Instead I'd contemplated drinking all day. I told myself that I'd been so good that it was time for a drink.

So I went to the trailhead, smoked my cigarette, and rode around the parking lot. I fully intended that to be the extent of my riding for today. *Dang, what if he checks my odometer?* So off I went, telling myself that I could drink if I wanted to after this, but I had to ride first. *New rule: ride first, then drink.*

This time I rode fifteen miles and was pretty proud of myself. I had biker's high! I was so excited to tell Craig that I forgot to buy any booze on the way home. *Oh well, tomorrow.*

After sharing the news, I practically skipped all the way to the shower. Maybe I was going to be a cyclist after all! While in the shower I thought about how all the cyclists I observed were skinny. Maybe that would be me!

I was in the kitchen eating a bowl of cereal—after all, I'd just burned an insane number of calories—when Craig ducked in and asked me to come outside. I went out to the garage to see the hatch of my vehicle open and my bike lying in the back on a blanket. I wasn't sure how to react to this latest development.

"There," he said. "Now you don't have to wait for me to get home with the truck. You can go to different trails and ride all day!"

Talk about pushy. *Thanks, buddy*, I thought. *Just what I want to do. Ride all day.*

Fifty-one days later I left on the Ride4Life. Hung over.

PART 2

OVERWHELMED

4

Miles of Misery

I can do this, I can do this. I repeat over and over to myself as I watch the team start to ride out of the parking lot. Friends and family start to cheer louder, and all the hype makes me feel like an ever bigger fake. If they knew my secret they wouldn't cheer for me. My heart feels like it's going to pound out of my chest as I carefully clip into my pedals and push off with my left foot. I don't dare steal one last look at my hubby or I will lose any remaining resolve, and this facade of Sherry the Road Rider will be over. My fears are robbing me of a moment that should be exhilarating and exciting.

Instead, my thoughts are racing into the usual paranoia that follows a few days of binge drinking. *Does Craig know about my binging last night? Can anyone tell how hungover I am? Am I still drunk? What if I get sick while we're riding?* The questions are all justified. It's not just panic mode I'm in here. I had binged not only last night but for the three days leading up to the starting gate! While making homemade granola I was drinking vodka in my coffee mug. Now I am hungover, nauseated, and shaking. Not a good way to start a cross-country bike trek.

We ride out of the parking lot one by one. Everyone else is sailing out with a combination one-arm victory salute and wave. Not me. I don't want to be the one to crash into the person in front of me before we are even out of the parking lot. Instead

23

I attempt something resembling a quick hand gesture of some kind, not daring to let go for more than a second. *One pedal stroke at a time. You got this. One pedal stroke at a time. You got this.*

My odometer tells me we are at the one-mile mark. *I only have to do that 1,199 more times. OK, wrong thought process. Think one mile at a time.* I also note that my odometer totals seven hundred miles. I am about to ride more in ten days than I had in the last fifty-one days.

I steal a glance behind me to see how everyone else is doing.

I hardly know any of the other riders. We'd ridden together for a few organized rides, but that was about it. Now we are spending the next twelve days together—should prove interesting. We are a quiet group for the first hour of riding. I'm sure everyone is thinking about the long journey ahead, just like me. I am thankful to the bottom of my bike shoes that, so far, I am keeping up with the pace.

At around mile fifteen we have our first break stop. We arrive in Saugatuck, a sleepy little lakeshore town known for its fun bars and restaurants. Not today. I am stopping in as cyclist Sherry, foolishly riding my bicycle from Michigan to Texas. It is a totally surreal feeling to be here in this mode and not as an evening barfly. The gas station we are stopping at on the side of the road had not even been on my radar before. I refill both of my water bottles right away. I'd already drank a lot of water for riding such a short distance. The SAG (Support and Gear) team puts out snacks but I can't eat, even though I know I need to. I am dehydrated and desperately need to keep pounding water. The women line up for the bathroom right away. I don't have to pee but am feeling nauseated, so I take my turn.

As I dry heave in that smelly gas-station restroom I promise myself, *I will never, never, never again.* Just like I had a thousand times before, but this time I think the vow might stick. *I must never forget how miserable I am in this moment.* I'm the last one out of the restroom and it's up to me to return the key on the wooden stick to the clerk inside. I swallow hard to overcome the smell of hotdogs on the roller grill and stale tobacco that fills the air in the small station. I inhale the fresh air when I come out and realize I had been holding my breath for the few moments I was inside. I hurry over to my bike and rejoin the group that appears to be waiting for me. This would be the trend throughout most of the ride. I always seemed to be the last one ready to go.

At our second break stop about forty miles in, I write in the little leather journal I keep on my bike: *This will work*. However I am coping with all this, it's working.

I'd spent the last twenty-five miles praying like never before. Selfish prayers—all about me—to feel better, to make it through this day, to not get sick. Me, me, me. I am so sick of myself, and I suspect God must be too.

I am finally able to eat a banana and down some Gatorade. Things are looking up, my nausea subsides somewhat, and I am feeling a little more confident by midday. I am keeping the pace along with everyone else. When it is finally lunchtime I am actually ready to eat. *Carbs, please! What will our SAG team be serving for lunch?* I am hoping for sandwiches, maybe fresh fruit and cookies. *Oh my gosh, Subway sounds amazing! Bread—just give me bread!*

Everyone digs out the bag chairs that we had brought for our longer stops. I sink into mine and let it surround my fatigued lower half. I sit back and wait to be served. Imagine my surprise and disappointment when Mark comes out of the motorhome with two loaves of generic white bread, a jar of peanut butter, and a beach towel to put his meager offering on.

Seriously? Jesus fed the five thousand with a spread better than this! Where was the platter of cheese and cold cuts I had been dreaming about the last ten miles? The soft bakery bread and chocolate chip cookies? The fruit bowl of mangoes and grapes? Obviously that daydream would not be coming true.

I steal a glance at my buddy Carolyn, and we exchange a look of disbelief. Oh well, it's food and I'm starving, so I get in line for the community knife and make myself a sandwich,

25

vowing to buy cookies at the next gas station. Even one of the roller dogs that had sickened me this morning was starting to sound appetizing! At least cleanup is easy: crumbs shaken off the towel, twist-tie fastened on the leftover bread, and empty peanut butter jar thrown away. Reminds me of a daycare picnic.

The afternoon passes quickly. I feel rejuvenated by peanut butter and the beauty of riding along the lakeshore. The first day we are all full of adrenaline, which has to help. Then our energy starts to wear off around five p.m., or about eighty miles in with thirty-four miles to go.

The first day is long and hot. My body is being worn down and so is my mind, and I let the negativity from the morning creep back in. I cannot imagine how I am going to do this over and over again for the next twelve days.

We're supposed to be on the last ten miles of the day, but I'm sure we're lost in the middle of nowhere without a big city the size of Valparaiso, our stop for the night, in sight. I'm new to this and don't realize we're taking the back way into the city to avoid the busy roads. Then we crest a hill and Valparaiso appears like a mecca in the desert (except it's Indiana). The group cheers and fist-pumps. It had been a long twelve-hour day on our bikes, and we are tired. We had ridden 114 miles! I have never in my life been so happy to see a two-star hotel. I want to kiss the ground and go to bed.

Not so fast. First things first: we have to carry our bikes up to our rooms, come back down and grab our luggage, shower, and find dinner. I also want to call Craig and let him know that I'm safe. These days are hard for him, too, worrying about his wife on the road all day.

I'm excited to call him and share the day's achievement, but by the time I make the call all my enthusiasm vanishes. I start to cry the moment he answers. "Please come get me," I beg. He refuses, so I kind of hang up on him. OK, I *do* hang up on him. I am beyond angry—I always have to blame someone else for these messes I get myself into. This one is definitely his fault.

He's the one that bought this stupid bike and pushed me too far in the first place. He should come get me. Any adrenaline high I had an hour earlier when we rode in is completely gone. Once again, I feel defeated and totally incapable of doing this again tomorrow. *Stay in the moment. One thing at a time. You got this.*

I cry for a bit while taking a much-needed shower and try to pull myself together. No time for lingering in a shower of self-pity though; everyone is waiting for me, as usual. Good Lord, don't any of these women wear makeup? Forced to skip my usual getting-ready ritual, I join my impatient group in the lobby and we walk to dinner across the street. There we eat a record amount of food, totally making up for our meager peanut butter picnic (hence no weight loss on this trip, even though we are burning an average of five thousand calories a day).

The meal is enjoyable as long as I don't look in the mirror on the wall directly across from me. I don't even recognize the woman I see in the reflection, with her swollen, sunburnt face and frizzy, damp hair. I look hideous, but then again so does everyone else.

As tired as we are, the mood is still pretty high. We successfully completed the first day! Most of us had ridden farther today than ever before. There's a lot of laughter as we share stories with the SAG team and they with us. I mock Mark about his gourmet lunch and tell him to up his game tomorrow. As I laugh I feel a new hope growing—a bit of hope that this might actually be a little fun at times.

It would be more fun with a little of that. I gaze longingly at the bar. I am pretty sure this isn't a drinking group. In fact I *know* this isn't a drinking group. For once I quickly let go of that thought. Drinking doesn't even sound that great, and I take note that I am kind of having fun while sober—a new experience for me.

Dinner also has a sad undertone; we have to say goodbye to Derek. He is only joining us for the first day of the ride, as his wife is about to have a baby. She drove to Valparaiso to join us for dinner and to take Derek home. I desperately want to go back to Holland with them, but my mouth won't open to ask. I'm trying to catch Derek's eye so I can cast my silent plea to save me and take me home. He doesn't see it, and I have to work hard not to cry when they leave. *Did anyone else wish they were going home, or is it just me? Probably just me.*

We head back to the hotel for a quick meeting about the morning routine and prayer. I go to bed slathered with Monkey Butt rash cream wherever it is needed (everywhere) and cry silently into my pillow so my roommate Carolyn won't hear me. I know tomorrow will be harder, as I have been through this before. The detoxing. The second day is always the worst. There will be shaking and nausea, and I will be on a bike. All day.

Lord, help me. In spite of my "never, ever again" mantra at the gas station this morning, I want a drink—badly. The thought alone devastates me. As bad as that moment had been, here I am again. Just like any other time I tried to quit, a drink seems like a good idea at the end of the day. Thankfully, I am so fatigued I'm not able to stay awake long enough to dwell on the cravings.

The night brings me a pleasant surprise. Usually when I'm not drinking and for a few nights after I experience a three a.m. alarm clock of anxiety-induced panic and night sweats. Not tonight. I sleep like a rock, and when my alarm blares at six a.m., I wake up smiling. I feel elated that I did not suffer through the early morning anxiety of detoxing. Then I realize where I am and quit smiling.

5

Merry Christmas, Baby

Day two of Ride4Life is hot—unbearably hot. The destination is Crawfordsville, Indiana, a daunting one hundred and five miles away. At the first break I stand in the motorhome to cool off and guzzle water. By lunchtime I am lying on the bench table in the motorhome whining to Carolyn about how miserable I am. Carolyn had gotten off her bike and taken charge of the SAG team. Already our meals are better. She knows what we need in this heat, and it's not stale bread and peanut butter. She understands that eating is necessary but hard when it is so hot. Fruit is our new best friend. It is cool, refreshing, and full of carbs to help us keep going.

I don't know if my nausea is from the heat or the hangover, but it is bad. My stomach rebels and I keep dry heaving in the motorhome's bathroom, praying no one can hear me. I don't understand how I am guzzling so much water and not throwing it up. I must be severely dehydrated.

When I climb back on my bike to join the others, it is the worst heat of the day and none of us are looking forward to this next leg. I have a sun rash on my legs for the first time in my life. My skin tone is quite dark, so that usually doesn't happen to me. Is it crazy that I am proud of those red bumps on my shoulders and legs? It's like an external badge of suffering for all to see. I'm so self-absorbed—all about me and my sun rash.

If I really want sympathy, I should show them my butt, but nobody wants to see that. Just saying—it's not pretty. Every time I get on my bike, the first few miles are so painful, and then slowly the discomfort goes away. I think it becomes bearable because the discomfort of the heat makes me forget about everything going on in my lower half—aka legs and butt. Sometimes I don't want to stop for breaks simply because I don't want to start the painful process all over again.

Late afternoon hits and we are starting to struggle, a repeat of the day before. The pace slows, and the group is quiet. I can almost see everyone get lost in his or her own thoughts, leaving me time to think as well. The first twenty-five miles this morning had also been quiet. It's crazy how my thought process is so different in the afternoon when I am hot and tired.

In those first few morning miles I had felt so close to God. We had left as the sun was rising, and my eyes had filled with tears as I thanked God for answering my prayers to bring me into sobriety. In the morning that's where I was—sobriety. Day two! Never drinking again! I loved using that time to pray while I rode in the morning, just like I had in my training. My morning conversation with God usually went something like this.

> *Dear Lord,*
>
> *Thank you for the beauty of your creation that I am witnessing this morning. Thank you for each and every person I am riding with—and our SAG drivers. Protect us all and keep us out of harm's way. Be with my husband and children, and thank you for the love and support they have shown me. Thank you for my strong legs that keep going round and round. Thank you for loving me and believing in me when I don't even believe in myself. Lord, help this desire to stay sober always be as strong as it is right here in this moment.*

The afternoon conversation goes a little differently.

> *Dear God,*
>
> *Please bring some clouds to hide this blasted, hot sun. I mean, it's gorgeous and all, but it's so freaking hot! Also, please no more hills today. I just can't do it. I'm tired and feel so beaten up. My body is shot. How did you ever think I could do this in the first place? Please, God, take away the pain I have been sitting on for the last ninety miles. If you make it go away, I promise I'll never drink again—or at least not until I get home. Also, Lord, please bless my family. Speaking of family, do they care how miserable I am right now? A text would be nice, but they are all caught up in their own worlds, I'm sure. They don't give a crap about me. Nobody does. Sorry, God, didn't mean to go off on a tangent!*

This seems to be a pattern in my life—bargaining with God to get me out of seemingly hopeless situations. It never works, but I keep trying. This seems to be the theme for my life thus far, from when I was a little girl all the way into my mid-forties. Screw up first and then try to talk my way out of whatever I got myself into. Sometimes it works, but most times it doesn't. If I were God, I certainly would not listen to any of my negotiating. I have yet to keep any of the frequent promises I make to him when asking him to get me out of whatever trouble I'm in.

As I ride I think back to the troubling time that still brings me shame and guilt almost eight months later. Truly my lowest moment in my drinking career. A time when I pleaded once again for God to get me out of a mess. Back then I had hurt my family deeply and promised to quit drinking. Are they aware of the lie I have been living for the past eight months?

ೞೞೞೞ

December 26, 2009

We were going to my dad's house to celebrate our family Christmas. I don't remember much about the time before we left for the party, but I do know I had been secretly drinking throughout the day. As usual.

In my mind, drinking while I took down the Christmas decorations made a mundane task I strongly disliked a little more tolerable. I have never been a fan of Christmas decorations. They mess up my house and make things feel cluttered. Glitter—who invented that? So yes, I am that person who takes down all the decorations the day after Christmas.

Around four p.m. I passed out, which was typical after a day of drinking. My husband came home and woke me up, assuming I had just been napping. This screwed up my drinking. I never wanted to appear drunk, just relaxed. I had a method for this madness and it required small amounts of alcohol over the course of the day. While getting ready to go I pounded a few shots of vodka in my closet, ignoring my own rules set to prevent myself from overimbibing. On the way to my dad's, I remember thinking that it wasn't enough, and my body and mind wanted more.

When we got to my dad's I made myself a small drink, which appeared to others to be lasting a long time. But when no one was looking I poured shot after shot into my glass.

At some point, in the middle of the party, I passed out. When I woke up, everyone was gathering their things and it was quiet, so quiet. No one was listening to me as I tried to make excuses about falling asleep. I was just hustled out the door. I only have a brief memory of leaving that night. I remember kneeling down behind the bar to "refresh" my drink and then waking up in our bed the next morning with a feeling of dread that something was very wrong. I had experienced my worst blackout yet.

I lay there with my back to my husband, my mind racing, frantically trying to remember the events of the night before.

What have I done? How bad is the damage? How much have the kids seen? It was so quiet I questioned whether my husband was even lying next to me.

Finally I worked up the courage to speak. "It's bad, isn't it?"

"Yes," Craig said, and without another word he got up and left me there, closing the door behind him.

I felt like I had been punched in my gut, I was hurting so badly. My grief was so severe over how I had hurt my family that I felt physical pain. I pleaded to God, "Please just take this away! Rescue me, save me from myself and the destruction I have brought to my family." Not once in that dark hour did I ask him to help me quit drinking. I didn't want that; I just wanted to better control it, and if I couldn't then I needed to get better at hiding it until I could control it. When this is your thought process, you know you're sick.

My entire family had witnessed their wife, daughter, mother, sister, and aunt fall down in a drunken stupor and ruin a family Christmas. There would not be a do-over. Christmas 2009 would always be remembered as the one I had ruined with my drinking, and there was no taking that back. The damage was done, but I still thought I could keep drinking. It wasn't on my radar that I had to *quit*.

After my tears were exhausted, I showered and decided to face the music and make amends. I tried to use makeup to hide the dark circles under my eyes, to no avail. Nor was there anything I could do about the puffy bloat my face seemed to be carrying around more lately. I went downstairs and cautiously approached my youngest daughter where she was lying on the living room couch pretending to watch TV. Olivia was fourteen years old and the only one of our children still living at home. I sat down next to her. "Hi."

She put on a forced smile. "Hey, Mom."

I started to launch into an apology for the events of last night, but she cut me off right away "Mom, it's OK." She said it with a fake smile and glistening eyes. Since Olivia obviously didn't want to discuss it, I gave her a hug and looked for my next victim to apologize to. I found him in the basement, sitting in the dark staring stonily at the wall.

When I stood in front of Craig, he wouldn't even look at me.

I started to cry. "I am so sorry, honey." Usually at this point he would comfort me, say the right thing, give me a hug. Not this time. He just stared straight ahead and still wouldn't look at me. His jaw was firmly set, and he was angry—angrier than I had ever seen him before. It ripped me apart inside when I looked him in the eyes. All I could see was pain—all caused by me. I had not only hurt him for the hundredth time; I had hurt our kids. Forgiveness would not come easy. He had worked so hard to protect our kids from my drinking. As parents we will do anything to protect them, and he had so far succeeded. Until last night had spiraled out of his control and I had committed the ultimate sin. I had hurt our children. When that happens we as parents are known to roar like lions at whatever or whomever has hurt them.

When he did speak, it was a quiet roar. He proceeded to give me a play-by-play of the previous evening's events. He left nothing out. He didn't try to downplay the sequence of events. "Your mouth was offensive. You passed out in the middle of opening gifts. I had no explanation for the rest of the family as they watched you, in a drunken stupor, be a complete jerk."

I tried to interrupt and he held up his hand. "My turn!" With a shaking voice he continued. "I finally told them to ignore you. You slept and we tried, unsuccessfully I might add, to finish the party. Can you even fathom what that was like? Trying to celebrate Christmas with an elephant in the room—a drunken elephant?"

By the time Craig ended his narrative of how the night had unfolded, I was on the floor with my head on his knees, sobbing uncontrollably. I finally felt his hands on my head, and then he buried his face in my hair and said, "No more. Please, no more. You have to quit. I'll do whatever I can to help you, but there cannot be any more alcohol, *ever*."

My heart was breaking for how much I had put him through, and I desperately wanted to tell him what he wanted to hear. So I did. "Never again. Never again, babe. I promise." All the while my mind was screaming. *HOW? I don't know how to do life without alcohol! I don't even know where to start. Help me, God. Please, help me! I don't know how to do this.*

As we stood up together and hugged, he promised that he would be with me every step of the way, and I believed him. I just didn't know what good it would do. Later that day I tried to make amends with my two older children. They were running a gauntlet of emotions. Hurt, anger, and—surprisingly—they were both shocked as well. Of course, they knew I occasionally drank too much, but for the most part I had hid it and Craig had covered for me.

Those days were over. I told everyone what they wanted to hear. No more drinking, it would never happen again. Never mind *how* it would never happen again—I would deal with that part later. I would be under a microscope from now on, my family watching for the least little clue that I had been drinking. This worried me. I would definitely have to reassure them by my actions that I was behaving. After a while they would move on and not worry about it anymore, and I could figure out how to be more discreet.

The next morning I had breakfast with my dad and bawled like a five-year-old. My dad is my hero, and knowing that I had let him down was hard for me to face. But my dad is a man of grace. He reminded me of how much he loved me and that he didn't think any worse of me for having a drinking problem. That I was strong and had both a lot of support and—most importantly—many reasons to get sober and stay sober.

I went on to tell my mom and stepdad what had happened at Christmas. More tears were shed and promises of support were made. Then I went to a post-Christmas brunch with my girlfriends from high school and filled them in as well. Everyone was encouraging, and in no way did I feel judged for my addiction.

"What can we do to help?" they all asked.

"I don't know," I replied. "I've never done this before either." I told them that I couldn't go to our upcoming girls' weekend because there would be drinking. We had been friends for over thirty years, and we loved to go away and have fun. We would drink and laugh harder than should be possible. We might not be eighteen anymore. but we sure knew how to have a good time.

We were past the days of bar-hopping and loud places where we couldn't hear each other. We would usually rent a condo and get some wine and good food and catch up for hours. Now that they had heard my confession, I could no longer drink in front of them. They insisted we could go ahead with our plan but we just wouldn't drink. Noble idea, but I was sure I would be the miserable one missing drinking the most.

There was a deep sadness within me and I knew where it was coming from: a place of guilt and shame for being a fraud and a liar. When I told everyone I had quit drinking, there was some truth there. I had been sober since December 28, 2009. It was now the beginning of January, I was almost two weeks in, and it wasn't getting any easier. I had every intention of drinking again as soon as it was "safe." When the conditions were a little more favorable that I would not get caught. When I would only hurt myself and no one else. I didn't know when that day would be, but I knew it would come.

Another part of that deep sadness came from leaving a big part of my life behind. When I shared with friends and family that I was an alcoholic, I was closing the door on ever drinking with them again. All my drinking would have to be done in secret from now on. Life would never be the same. What would this do to so many of my relationships? Everything was going to change.

6

Two Truths and a Lie

I slowly get to know other people on this ride. A fascinating way to pass time on the bike is inviting someone to talk about themselves. One rider, Don, is a small-town dentist with more stories than I would have ever believed possible. We pass miles playing Two Truths and a Lie. Don has a hard time coming up with the lie and, unbeknownst to him, I have an even more difficult time coming up with the truths! This is a game I would not recommend anyone play with me. Simply because I will win. It involves lying, deceit, and conniving, and I am a master of all three in real life.

ಶಂಶಂ

January 2010

Truth: I would go to an AA meeting at noon every day. Then I could report to Craig all the things I learned that day. I would share stories about the people at the meeting, playing along with the rules of AA and only using other attendees' first initial for anonymity. I would emphasize the hardships they had, thus making my little drinking problem look very tame compared to what others were up to.

That is where the truth would end and lies came into play. Mostly by omission but still lies. I didn't enlighten Craig that after the meeting I would sometimes wander the mall aimlessly until Olivia was due to come home from school. I wanted to avoid being home alone with a long, sober afternoon ahead. There was also the anticipation of what I might find in my explorations, which was a new high for me, feeding my "what can I get away with if it isn't drinking?" state of mind.

This was a dangerously expensive way to pass the time. I soon began to accumulate many things I didn't need. It was my new rush, my new way to a high: retail therapy. I wasn't happy with my body and always looked for the perfect item of clothing to camouflage my alcohol-induced bloat and weight gain.

Let me just point out the unfairness of that. Whenever I saw women in the end stages of their drinking, they were thin! Cutting out an extra two thousand calories a day of alcohol should have been having a profound effect on my weight, but it wasn't. At least not in the weight-loss department—instead I was slowly gaining weight! So no matter what I bought, I wasn't happy with how it looked and never ended up wearing most of it.

This led to lie number two, the one I told myself. I continually bought a smaller size of clothing than what I currently wore. I would find something that I really liked, try it on, and then ponder how much better it would look once I lost weight. *Hmmm*, I would think as I looked at it from all angles in the dressing room mirror. *I should buy a smaller size because I am losing weight (I mean, I am going to), and then this fabulous dress would be such a waste and just hang in my closet, reminiscent of my fat days.* I definitely wanted to enjoy this piece for years to come. So I would go back out to the floor and buy it in the next smaller size. Empowered by my latest weight-loss inspiration in the shopping bag on my arm, I would saunter to the food court. I would carefully choose a fattening treat or two (usually sugar-related) to binge on because the next day I was starting a *major* diet.

Now I had two new adrenaline rushes: shopping and sugar. Both filled the emptiness about as long as alcohol did and came with guilt and regret—just like alcohol did. All that I had to show for my latest high was a closet full of clothes that didn't fit and a muffin top. I see now that I was lying not only to Craig about what my day really looked like but also to myself. I told myself that these purchases and treats would make me happy. Even planning to lose weight was invigorating, but quite often the next day I would find myself doing the exact same thing as the day before.

Truth: Went to AA meeting.
Lie: Went shopping and binged on sugar.

Evenings were the hardest to get through. My days always started with renewed determination. It felt so good to get a full night's sleep and not wake up with a hangover. Why would I ever drink again? I felt wonderful! The birds were singing, the sunrise was beautiful, and I was full of gratitude. I went about my morning tasks like freaking Pollyanna playing the glad game. I was always eager to attend the noon meeting and often went in high spirits.

The meeting would often drag me down. My thoughts would become darker, and I would question my ability to stay sober forever. *Forever?* It wasn't possible. No matter what people said at the AA meetings, I couldn't apply that saying to me! I needed to think much further ahead than "one day at a time." Didn't they know how ridiculous that sounded? I could say "one day at a time" until I was blue in the face, but I was too smart to be fooled by that ridiculous line. They meant *forever* and I wasn't buying into their story.

By the time my husband got home from work, I'd be climbing the walls. I think we went to about ten movies in three weeks. Once I was settled into a theater seat with my jumbo popcorn and Milk Duds, I could lose myself for about two hours to the screen in front of me. Then, by the time I got home, I could pop some Ambien and go to bed. I would wake up filled with gratitude for having made it through another night. Then the whole process would start all over again.

Those days would have been easier if I had put more effort into accepting that I wasn't going to drink again. I just couldn't wrap my head around it! There was too much ahead of me in life to comprehend not drinking. Weddings, trips, anniversaries, girls' weekends. What if someone I love died? Surely there must be exceptions to this "no alcohol forever" rule that everyone but me agreed was the only way to stay sober. I left every AA meeting disappointed, always hoping that maybe someone would share a method other than "forever"—you know, when allowances were made. Didn't happen, of course.

In late January my ninety-year-old grandma ended up in the hospital. She had a painful neck surgery and had to be in a neck brace for several months. I loved my grandma very much, and it was hard to see her in pain and uncomfortable.

My cousin and I spent a lot of time at her side that week. On that Friday I left the hospital, drove straight to the liquor store, and bought a fifth of vodka. I told myself I deserved this. I was sure that just about the whole world was having happy hour, and I intended to as well. The past week had been hell, and nobody could possibly understand how I was feeling. If they didn't understand, they shouldn't be able to tell me what to do. So, I would not enlighten anyone about my decision to engage in happy hour along with the rest of the world.

My happy hour looked a little different from everyone else's though. Mine was for a party of one and happened in the corner of my dark closet, and the whole time, I was gripped with paranoia that my husband would find out. My appetizer was a few spoonsful of peanut butter to hopefully mask the smell of any alcohol on my breath. When I didn't get caught, I foolishly congratulated myself for my achievement in drinking successfully (not getting caught equated success).

I had lied to everyone the past few weeks, but at least I'd been honest with myself. I knew I wasn't done drinking. When and if I quit, it would be on *my* terms and my terms alone.

I had achieved twenty-six days of sobriety, and it had been twenty-six of the hardest days of my life. I was relieved it was over so I could move back into the life I was used to: a life of hiding and lying my way through each day just so I could drink.

༄༅༄༅

Ride4Life, Day 2

Why would God listen to my pleas? I wasn't ready to change, and he knew it. So by the end of day two, I'm *done* praying for God to help me. I would do this bike ride by myself in my own will. After all, my own will had gotten me into this mess in the first place; now it would have to get me through.

I'd done hard things on my own before—like the spring break cruise we had just taken. I'd stayed sober for a whole week! No small achievement when you're surrounded by booze everywhere you turn. Granted, I had tried to drink, but alcohol wasn't free, you couldn't pay cash for anything, and I couldn't risk a drink showing up on our tab.

But one day we went ashore for an excursion. In a moment of bravery (or possibly stupidity), I snuck away from my group and bought some rum on one of the islands, stowing it safely in my purse. The victory was short-lived. While approaching the ship to reboard, I saw staff checking the passengers' bags for booze. I quickly ran off the dock to a bathroom to throw the rum away before I was publicly shamed. It almost killed me to leave it there. I couldn't even guzzle some down because I didn't have any gum to hide the smell on my breath. As the ship left the port, I watched the little blue shack—where I had thrown away my last chance to drink for three more days—fade into a small dot. The frustration killed me! I was a real jerk those last three days.

Although that cruise didn't physically compare to this bike ride, it had been hard. It wasn't easy to contain the rage and frustration that wanted to burst out of me like a scene from

The Exorcist. Try doing that on a ship for a week—in a room the size of my master bathroom. I swear those rooms are the main reason people drink so much on cruises. It had never bothered me on any other cruise, but then again I had been wasted for most of them.

I'd already been busted a few times by my husband since I first broke my sobriety record of twenty-six days in January. So after the cruise, I was living for Monday—the day they all went back to school and work and I would be blessedly alone for the day. I took full advantage of my alone time and was wasted by noon, slept away the afternoon, and was sobered up before anyone got home. I went to bed with every intention of a new Day One on Tuesday. I'd just had to get drinking out of my system.

By the end of the second day of biking, my own will has about run out and I'm exhausted. I tried to shake off the bad memories and concluded that I couldn't keep going down the path of shame and regret, but in reality I needed to be reminded of how much I'd hurt my family—and of my vow to never hurt them again. As we pedal into Crawfordsville, Indiana, with our crappy hotel in sight, a sign reading "Welcome to Crawfordsville—Home of Ben Hur" greets us.

Lord help me.

PART 3

BEWILDERED

7

Love Notes

"Off to Effingham!" It sounds to me like our fearless leader, Mark, is swearing at us as we take off on this hot dusty morning. He isn't, it's just the name of our destination today. I, however, repeat *Effingham* like a swear word in my head. It kind of sounds like "Effing Ham." You see where this is going.

As much as I complain, these first few miles of the day are always the best. The beauty of the sunrise is mingling with the cool morning air. I'm grateful to be starting out with my usual morning exuberance. This is the third day and I'm over the detox hump, albeit a bit smug that I just detoxed on my bike for the last couple hundred miles and have, so far, lived to tell about it. Not that I'm telling anyone. I may be sore in unmentionable places, but compared to the shakes and nausea of the first two days I feel like a rock star.

I make up my own song to the tune of "I Am Sixteen Going on Seventeen," from *The Sound of Music* as I listen to the soundtrack on my iPod to start the day. "I have gratitude, I have strong legs, merry am I on my bike. I am a rock star, I am a rock star, but I still cannot sing."

I'm feeling carefree, almost giddy. Later in the morning I sing "My Angel Is a Centerfold" by the J. Geils Band to my riding buddies. As I belt out the words, I realize this song is a little sketchy for the Christian group. Too bad. We could use a little fun here and I felt it was up to me to make it happen. Besides, it's not like they're going to send me home for singing a song that's a little risqué. But when "Highway to Hell" comes on I keep it to myself, although the other riders might be amused by that because the hills we encounter later that day go well with the song. "Highway to Hell" matches my mood whenever another unbelievable climb in elevation appears.

I most look forward to the familiar ding alerting me that I have a text, even though I can't read it until the next break. Texting and biking is frowned upon (as I found out early in the ride). To pass the time I make up stories in my head about who the text is from and what they are texting me about.

Most often the first text of the day is my husband, to start my day on my bike with some sort of positive affirmation. Craig's not big on texting, but he's sent me a few simple words these past two mornings to let me know he was thinking of me.

I check my phone at our first break stop to make sure I haven't missed anything. Not one single new text. *Great, I've been forgotten already. Craig is probably celebrating his freedom. Maybe even giddy that it's someone else's turn to watch me. Well, that didn't take long.*

Maybe my whole family is getting together while I'm gone and going to one of our favorite restaurants we've been avoiding because it has a bar I had frequented. Or maybe they are all coming over for steaks. Craig will grill up our prize rib eyes with Texas toast. The guys will hang out by the grill popping the tops off cold, frosty beers. My oldest daughter will most likely take over my kitchen, along with my wine glass, and be busy making mashed potatoes while the other two girls sit at the kitchen bar sneaking sips from the wine glass while my oldest pretends not to notice.

"I propose a toast," Craig will say, raising his glass. "God bless Mom today as she rides across the state on day three of the trip. I am grateful she is sober today and someone else's problem." They will all shout "Hear, hear," clink their glasses together, and laugh at Craig's incredible wit.

I am famous for creating scenarios that don't exist. This one is about as big a creation as I can dream up. We don't drink with our kids. My oldest has never taken over my kitchen or drunk wine in my kitchen. The only possible truth in that scenario is the rib eyes. I use every moment on my bike during the latter part of the morning to create big lies until I'm jolted out of my negative fantasy when someone blows a tire.

Now, when someone blows a tire, I just stand off to the side and wait while team testosterone goes to work. For some reason unbeknownst to the female mind, this appears to be a way for my male counterparts to prove their manhood. They all want a role in fixing said tire. I usually choose to take advantage of the unexpected break to check for texts and new comments on my Facebook page. I'm interrupted from my technology break when one of the guys yells, "Hey, does anyone have an extra tube?" Seizing the opportunity to finally be of assistance I quickly pocket my phone and rifle through the bag on my bike.

This bag can hold as much as any TSA-approved carry-on. Among all my supplies, I know I have a tube. I dig through lipstick, sunscreen, extra socks, powder, Monkey Butt cream, a hairbrush, hairspray, journal and pen, and finally come up with a bike tube.

A couple of the guys are staring at me in disbelief.

"Hey, no judgment here. I found the tube, didn't I?" I said. As I start strategically fitting all the gear back in my bag, I see something. At the bottom of my bag is a note tightly folded into a little triangle with the word "hon" written on it. I know it is going to be special. Crying is inevitable; I feel the tears forming before I even open it. As I start unfolding it, I work hard to keep myself from sobbing. It's a love note from Craig, my man of few words, and the timing couldn't be better: "I love you. I'm proud of you. You are stronger than you realize. You got this, babe."

I feel so loved in this moment. I had spent the entire morning convincing myself that no one cares, no one loves me, that I have been gone for three days and forgotten. I had dug my own grave in the cemetery of the unlovable, but this note resurrects my belief in my hubby's love. It brings me back to life, a life where no matter how crappy I treat someone, they still love me.

The irony isn't lost on me. This is exactly how I've been taught that God loves me. Unconditionally. There isn't anything I can do to keep him from loving me. I reflect on this new realization. I can see God showing me through Craig that I am worth loving, and worth fighting for.

Do I believe I am worth fighting for? I ponder this question, and my conclusion saddens me—my honest answer is no. I'm so tired of fighting this losing battle with myself. Craig is willing to fight with me. He isn't going anywhere, but I had viewed him as the enemy. But seeing Craig's note, I know it's time to ask for help in this daily battle I keep losing.

Even when I'm sober the battle is still raging. I will start by asking help from God and talking to him about it for the next twenty miles instead of walking (in this case riding) down the road of self-pity.

The flat is fixed and it's time to go again. Feeling empowered by my new attitude, I shove off for another twenty-mile stretch with Craig's note tucked where I can see it.

8

Highway to Hell

By the time we stop for lunch the temperature has risen dramatically, and on top of that we've acquired a challenging headwind. There are a few times I want to say, "Screw it!" and throw my bike in the motor home. But I don't follow through on that thought; I have way too much pride. I'm pretty sure no one at home really thinks I'm going to stay on the bike the whole time, so I'm determined to prove them wrong.

The heat on my already-sunburnt shoulders tells me that we're in for another scorching afternoon on the bikes. I'm no longer impressed with my sun rash. I pray for shadowing clouds to give me a break from the sun's harshness on my blistering shoulders.

I can see more roller coasters ahead. Hills. Big hills. Always a thrill to go down, but always a seemingly endless climb back up. And as the day goes on, the hills get even bigger. Or maybe I just become weaker. The sun and hills beat up our tired bodies, but somehow we always keep going. The day's progression is best described in song. It would start with the "Hallelujah Chorus" and end with "Highway to Hell."

My fellow rider Betty helps. She's often my inspiration. At seventy-three years old, she is doing this trip on an old, semi-rebuilt ten-speed. Wearing a long-sleeved shirt to protect her skin from the sun's harmful rays, Betty rides an average of fifty to eighty miles a day. She's a little slower than most of us, but we're more than happy to accommodate her pace. We're all quite noble about it and never complain.

Truthfully, if Betty isn't riding we go faster, and it's much harder for me to keep up. The guys are much stronger than us girls. I'm always elated when I see Betty getting her bike out to rejoin the group when we pull up to a break stop. It means a reprieve from the pace the men keep setting! I wonder if anyone else secretly feels this way. I'm sure they do, but no one is going to admit it!

I'm in beast mode by the time we get to the hotel around seven p.m. Another twelve-hour day on the bike and I am shot. Done. This hotel doesn't look promising. It's about one hundred years old—and not in a vintage, quaint, oh-that's-darling way. It stands alone and looks anything but inviting. I mean, there is nothing else around.

I may be a little picky, but I only want two things at the end of the day. A decent hotel and a good meal. Strike one on the hotel, and I don't see a restaurant in sight.

Morning comes far too quickly, and the route for the day is Effingham to Carbondale. More flatland and dry, dusty fields with nothing of interest growing in them. This feels like what surely will be one of the longest days of the trip for several reasons.

About midday we could see only blackness ahead. The one thing I know about storms in this part of the US comes from *The Wizard of Oz*. This isn't Kansas, but it's dry, dusty, and boring, thus making me a little suspicious of the stillness around me. I go from feeling grateful for no headwind to wishing for a little breeze so the air doesn't feel so ominous. This changes fast, and I mean really fast. In a matter of minutes we find ourselves in forty-mile-per-hour winds with pelting rain and hail.

My friend Barb is a tiny woman on a big bike. We had nicknamed her bike the "lead sled" simply because it weighed more than she did. She was a powerful little thing on that bike.

But now the winds are so strong that Barb begins to be pushed backward, while the rest of us are at a virtual standstill against the wind. When the motor home comes alongside us to point us to shelter, we open the door and throw in Barb and the lead sled.

We have another mile to ride before we reach a convenience store that offers a break from the rain and winds. By the time we get there the storm has all but passed, but it's still a downpour. We'll clearly be soaked for the rest of the day. Can you say extra chafing? We make good use of our unexpected break and load up on donuts and candy, both for now and later. Sugar helps. Always.

We ride wet the rest of the day. The heat and humidity come back with fury, making it impossible to dry out. I'm not sure if it's the rain or the way I'm profusely sweating that is keeping me drenched, but either way it's the worst kind of miserable I've ever known. I'm so relieved to get to the hotel that night that I don't even care that it's another crappy one. As long as it has a shower and a bed, I don't care.

Day five dawns, and I feel less than fresh. I slept horribly, and some of my essentials are still damp. The lumpy mattress circa 1970 and the flat-as-a-pancake pillow have left me tired, achy, and in a truly foul mood . I keep to myself at breakfast, afraid to open my mouth lest I expose the beast that wants to roar its protest about biking today—or any other day for that matter.

By the time we finish devotions and announcements, I feel more optimistic. Today we're leaving Illinois and crossing into Missouri. We'll do this by crossing the Mississippi! Now this is sounding a little more exciting than the flatlands of Illinois.

By midafternoon we finally see the Mississippi River bridge, and I can feel the group's collective adrenaline pick up. The bridge is massive even from far away and gets larger and larger as we approach. Barb is as strong a rider as any of us, but she is scared to death of crossing this bridge. I'm not exactly excited about it, but it's making things more interesting than the usual pedaling through cornfields turned cotton fields.

A few miles before we reach the bridge, a local news van approaches with the driver rolling down his window and shouting, "Hey, I've been trying to catch up with you! Can we get a quick interview?" We all stop on the side of the road, and I get to work. I'm grateful for all the touch-up supplies I've been carrying in my bike pack, including my husband's Detroit Tigers ball cap that will help with helmet hair.

To my disappointment, Mark decides to handle the interview without us. *Fine*, I think as I put my helmet back on and zip up my bag. *I guess I won't be needing these touch-up supplies right now.*

Mark instructs one of the other guys to lead us toward the bridge. "Don't worry, I'll catch up," Mark says reassuringly.

I'm not worried at all, Mark. Not at all. I am sure in a burst of testosterone leadership, you will show up just in time to lead us across. (Yes, sarcasm is my inner voice.)

I quickly forget about Mark and my missed opportunity for being in the spotlight as we continue toward the Mighty Mississippi! Our perspective on everything is different while riding a bike; that's one of the things I love about it. You notice and appreciate what you see so much more. The details on the bridge are amazing. I don't think I've ever looked so closely at the makings of a bridge. But not going to lie—I'm getting a little nervous myself.

It's time to cross and Mark catches up just in time to join us (as I predicted). Barb is in front of me, and I can tell she's nervous. I try to encourage her the best way I know how. I try to make her laugh as we climb, but she isn't having it. She has an iron grip on her handlebars and isn't looking to the right or left, like the rest of us. At the top of the bridge we stop (even Barb) at the "Welcome to Missouri" sign and snap a few pictures. I look over the edge at the roaring river and have to admit it feels surreal.

Highway to Hell

I'm riding my bike across the Mighty Mississippi! I want to hang over the side and fling my arms up and embrace a *Titanic* moment, yelling, "I'm on top of the world!" In this moment I am sober, looking down at the Mississippi. I've ridden my bike from Michigan to Missouri, and it feels amazing.

After the excitement of crossing the Mississippi, the day drags. We take a wrong turn and immediately get lost in the podunk town we'd been dumped into as we exited the bridge. The day is hot and sickeningly humid. Everything touching my body is stuck to me. The grippers on the shorts on my thighs feel like a handsaw tearing into my legs with every stroke of the pedals. My hands are going numb from gripping my handlebars so tightly—the roads are full of potholes. My list of complaints for God that afternoon is endless.

I'm sick of this ride. Why did I ever sign up for it? Why didn't I just go to meetings like a normal alcoholic? Why did I choose to do things the hard way? What I wouldn't give for a drink at the end of this day! To curl up in my bed at the fleabag hotel with a bottle of wine and a pack of cigarettes. Yes, cigarettes. Throw in a giant bag of peanut M&Ms and I am golden.

I don't carry through with my wishful thinking. Our hotel tonight is a lone building in a field. No party store in sight. Probably divine intervention.

Divine Appointment in
a Pizza Parlor

After a shower, and sporting my new look of no makeup and wet hair, I go to meet everyone in the lobby to decide on dinner. There are two choices for dinner in this town, if you want to call it a town: Chinese or pizza. The guys want Chinese food and the girls want pizza, so we split up. *It might be nice to have a girls' night.* We are getting closer as a team, and I look forward to dining with just the women.

I have this rule when scoping out a restaurant. If there aren't any cars in the parking lot during prime dinner hours, I give the place an immediate thumbs-down. My rule won't work here since our only other option is Chinese and joining the men. The thought of that smell (the food not the guys—OK, both smells) makes my stomach turn, so Italian for the ladies it is.

It's actually a cute little place. We sit down and try to hide our surprise when our waitress appears, and she's a sweet little girl about eight years old. This is clearly not her first rodeo; she's comfortable and tells us all about herself. With each word she speaks, my heart breaks for her a little bit more.

The first words out of her mouth, in her sweet southern drawl, are, "I like your shirt."

I'm wearing my blue shirt from Life Walk, another LPC fundraising event. It reads "Serving with the love of Christ."

Our waitress asks if we are from a church, and we explain what we're doing.

"Would you like us to send you a Life Walk T-shirt of your own?" I ask.

"I would like that very much. Can I have one for each of my sisters too?" she shyly responds.

A woman behind the counter, whom I assume is her mother, makes throat-clearing noises and raises her eyebrows. The little girl takes that as a hint to get our orders. "What would y'all like tonight?" With a little smile, she heads back to the kitchen.

Soon her parents are at our table, quizzing us about the ministry of LPC and the Ride4Life. What a wonderful family! Then they share their story. The woman tells us in a quiet voice, "Little Annie is actually my niece's daughter. My niece chose to have multiple abortions in the past, but for some reason she wanted to have the baby this time. She tried for a few months to be a mom to Annie, but she couldn't handle it. It wasn't long before she was back to her old lifestyle and then one day she was gone. We took Annie in and have been raising her as ours ever since. We eventually adopted her and now we are trying to adopt her two younger sisters as well."

There isn't a dry eye at our table as we listen to her talk. This is what LPC is all about. This is why we are riding. I'm humbled. This woman is doing more showing love to these little girls than I could ever do riding a bike for two weeks.

As we talk, the family's pastor walks in to pick up a pizza. After introductions and again explaining what we are doing, the pastor says, "I want to pray for you and for your ministry." On his way out he places a twenty-dollar bill at our table. "It isn't much, but I want to invest in what you are doing. God bless y'all."

This gesture and all the divine appointments we have found this evening floor us. We finish our pizza while Annie entertains us with an assortment of stories about her life. We are sorry to see the evening end, but in spite of how entertaining this little girl is, my eyelids are starting to droop.

When we try to pay the bill, the owner says, "The pizza is on us. We want to contribute somehow."

As we leave, we take a picture with Annie in front of, get this, a bicycle they have as a yard ornament. We return to the hotel spiritually and physically filled up from the evening. It's evident God had shown up.

At devotions that evening we share with the rest of the group what we had experienced. The guys share that they are feeling sick from the Chinese food. I'm glad the girls chose Italian food—for many reasons! When I call Craig, I try to convey the enormity of our dinner and what transpired, but I can't do the story justice.

I'm having an inner battle as I try to fall asleep. I've been with this group of riders for such a short time, and they don't really know me. If they did, I'm sure they wouldn't like me— I'm a fraud, a fake. I'm not like them. I'm Sherry, the drunk. What am I doing here? They think I'm one of them, but I know better. None of them have a secret sin like the one I carry with me every day.

I fall asleep praying, *God, rescue me. God, show me. God, use me. I want to be who these people think I am.* Instead of the prayers bringing me comfort, they leave me feeling hopeless. I'm just putting on another mask, being an actress in my own play. I'm not going to change. I know this. Yet there is curiosity: What if this is a pivotal moment in my life and I am on my way to a life in sobriety?

That thought scares the hell out of me. This bike trip is what I imagined rehab would be. The environment makes it impossible to drink, but what happens when I return to the real world with temptations swirling all around me? For me, instead of leaving the confines of a safe rehab building, it will be getting off my bike. I turn this fear over to God again and again as I finally fall asleep, for once feeling at peace about the days ahead.

PART 4

ENCOURAGED

10

Four Legs and Teeth

It's funny how quickly something can become routine. When I think about what my life looked like a week ago, there were similarities, but it had also drastically changed. Before, I would wake up at three a.m. and wonder what I had said or done the night before. Now I sleep like a dead person until the alarm blares at six a.m. and wake up stiff and sore but hangover-free.

Next comes the morning mental inventory of how I feel before I even move. Last week I would do a check for head pounding and nausea. Today I check my hands for stiffness and numbing and see if anything below the waist is screaming at me.

Last week I'd dress in exercise clothes and lay around in them all day. Today I'm putting on my bike shorts and actually using them for what they were made for! Last week I'd search for coffee, watching it perk with insane slowness. Now I'm getting on bike clothes, packing up my gear, checking bike tires, and doing group devotions while drinking my coffee. Before, I'd put on makeup to look human; now I no longer care if I look human because skipping makeup means a few more precious minutes of sleep.

So yes, my morning routine has changed, and I'm starting to embrace it. With the exception of those first few brutal minutes during those first few miles, spending a day on the bike is starting to trump a day at home with a hangover.

Today Mark announces that our destination is Wynne, Arkansas, about 116 miles away. I ask that we pray for no more dog chases. Seriously, I do. We have encountered a few dogs so far, but they've been of the friendly variety, more herding us along than actually chasing us. I'm fearful though; the road ahead looks a little like the scene from *Southern Comfort*, if you know what I mean. We start off with me cautiously optimistic and choosing to ride somewhere near the middle of the group instead of my usual spot in the back.

My fear of dogs is valid. I was raised with the gentlest of collies as family pets. But even the gentlest collie has been known to shed its loving personality and jump up and bite your friend's face. I'm not being dramatic—I witnessed this when I was ten years old. My collie, Laddie, had jumped up and bitten my young friend right above the eye for no apparent reason. This unexpected moment of Laddie-turned-Cujo is imbedded in my brain, solidifying my belief that there is not a dog around that I can trust completely.

My ten-year-old self has hung on to the fear of these four-legged beasts all the way into my forties. I grew up in the country and my main mode of transportation was my beloved purple bicycle. I rode my bike everywhere, and I mean everywhere. We are talking the 1970s here. A moment in time where there was no such thing as invisible fences and leashes. Country dogs ran as wild as we kids did.

Case in point: there were always *those* houses. The houses where the family dog owned the yard and, seemingly, the road in front of it. The house where said family dog could run loose and chase little girls with pink sponge rollers in their hair riding on banana-seat bikes. Being a street-smart country girl, I had developed a strategy to get past these houses without the ensuing dog chase. It was a three-step process involving assessment, visualization, and prayer.

My plan started with pulling over before riding past "dog houses" to get a visual on Rover's location. The best-case scenario would be catching a glimpse of him jogging around the house to the backyard. Then I could grab the window of opportunity and furiously pedal past its domain safely. If the dog was lying under a tree, I would pray that he was sleeping or that an adult would come outside. I didn't want any other kids to control the situation. Country kids were known to yell "Sic 'em!" and I had to prepare to be chased by the dog for their entertainment.

If I couldn't get a visual of the vicious beast, I proceeded cautiously, knowing there was always the possibility of a surprise attack. This occurred when the dog would slyly appear out of nowhere and I found myself in an unfair race because my opponent had four legs! The dog would race alongside me in the rows of corn with only a ditch separating me from imminent attack. Invariably the ditch would end, and I could only hope I was far enough ahead for the dog to give up the chase. I don't care if it was a German Shepherd or a rat terrier; they all had four legs and teeth.

Riding through Missouri on this country highway, I feel the same apprehension that I had as a little girl start to amp up. I review the strategies of my ten-year-old self, thinking they could be quite useful if my suspicions about what lie ahead prove true. I'm also repeating my verse for today, not because it was fitting—it was anything but fitting. I ruminate on the words, trying to make sense of it.

> Now it is God who has made us for this very purpose. . . . We live by faith, not by sight. . . . We make it our goal to please him. (2 Corinthians 5:5, 7, 9 NIV).

My interpretation goes something like this. *Really, God? This is my purpose? To ride my bike across the hottest, most boring states of America to be taken down by a rabid dog? I'm trying to have faith, but if I see a dog coming at me, the best way I can please you in this moment is to not let loose the four-letter words that will spew into my panic-driven mind and get me kicked off this ride.*

It isn't long before the inevitable happens and we become human prey. I spot the furry freight train approaching us at an unbelievable speed. "*Dog!*"

I frantically try to pop the safety top off the mace attached to my handlebars while my teammates yell, "No, stop! Don't do it—you're going to spray us!" I quickly realize my attempt at flattening the dog with chemicals is futile, so I resort to throwing the can at the dog. This works. This time.

I'm shaking so badly I want to cry. We still have a long way to go on these backroads of terror and this first chase sets the tone for the rest of the day. My biggest fear about the Ride4Life is coming to fruition. When I had started training, my angst had not been about getting hit by a car or taking a fall that would leave me laden with road rash. It was dogs. Those childhood memories were deeply ingrained. During training I'd tried to ride only on bike paths and in more populated areas. I had mostly managed to avoid the beasts, but there were a few times I was surprised by a four-legged chase, and my heart would pound out of my chest as I pedaled furiously to get away. Those chases always left me shaking, and I would go back to playing it safe and sticking to paths once again.

Our day unfolds into a pattern. We approach a small town, and in the early stages we're excited as we ride in, hoping for a gas station with a real restroom and snacks. On a trip like this it's the little things that keep us going. As we ride into said town, it's a sad encounter that we will see repeated along our journey. Much of the town is completely boarded up. Shut down. Families have abandoned homes and businesses and, many times, left something behind. This *something* being the family dog. These dogs find solace in one another, and it's not uncommon to see them in a pack, skinny and neglected. Many are pit bulls, which adds to the level of fear for some riders.

After the first few harrowing chases, we learn to ride quietly through each eerily silent shell of a former town. We study the dark recesses under the houses and see eyes. Sometimes the dogs chase us and other times they stay put. During the first few chases Mark yells, "Stay together!" *Hell no!* I channel my inner banana-seat, bike-riding little girl and furiously pedal to get away. "Just stay calm next time," the riders say. "There is strength in numbers. Stay together." I pretend to agree, knowing that I'll stick to my own method of escape.

I become agitated as we approach a questionable dog area, and my teammates are still laughing and talking. My inner child insists, *NO, you've got to be quiet! Believe me, I know how this works!* I give up on them and their inexperienced ways and start riding closer to the front of our own pack. They quickly learn to take their cue from me, as I take off like a launched rocket whenever I spot the enemy. My top speed was twenty-one miles per hour! This was on flat land, being chased by four-legged beasts who thought I was their lunch!

11

My Forrest Gump Moment

Day 7

Our destination today is Little Rock, Arkansas. Should it be a little surreal by now that I have ridden my bike to Little Rock all the way from Holland, Michigan? (Granted, we had sagged ahead at times in the interest of safety and we did not ride in the dark—no exceptions.)

I'm more than happy to leave the parking lot of the Starlite Motel. This one was by far the worst place we had stayed so far. It had a TV cable that ran through the shower and into a hole in the wall to get to the TV. My roommate, Carolyn, and I had quickly agreed not to turn the TV on, at least while the other one was showering. Also, my sheets had holes in them. I had chosen to sleep on top of the threadbare quilt. We all know what we think happens on those mangy bedcoverings, so I also decided to sleep fully clothed.

Late that night I heard voices outside and opened the door to see what was going on. It never occurred to me that there was anyone but my team staying in this infestation. Wrong. A pickup truck had backed up to my door with a bunch of guys leaning against it and sitting on the tailgate. They were obviously hardcore construction workers enjoying their own little happy hour.

We had a little stare-down, those workers and me. I know I looked pretty rough myself. They might have wondered if I was part of the road crew. I had a ten-second temptation to ask them for a beer, but I quickly rebutted that as the voice of reason quickly became loud—and won.

Carolyn and I decided we would not be opening our door again until morning. I put my bike in front of it for the night and slept with one eye open. When I woke up alive (but not well rested), I was grateful for an uneventful night and grateful I never had to see that place again.

We meet up in the parking lot for the usual routine of prepping the bikes and grabbing coffee. Except there isn't any. Coffee. This is a huge issue! Some of the others seem to be blowing it off like it's no big deal, but Barb and I feel differently. We take it upon ourselves to find gas station brew for us and a few of the others. It might delay our start time by a few minutes, but I consider it a necessary delay and so does Barb.

Our day starts out a little rough, but it just keeps getting better! We have a tailwind instead of the usual headwind. We ride like the wind! Literally. At lunchtime our SAG drivers find this little roadside stand where ladies are selling fresh fruit and various pickled items. We enjoy chatting with them, sampling their produce, and taking pictures with them before we leave.

I roll out of there thinking about something no one else is probably thinking about. I'm thinking about how social I had just been. It wasn't forced; I thoroughly enjoyed making the ladies laugh, and I even freely gave one of them a hug without thinking about it. I explore in my mind why I'm having these thoughts. It's confusing, but as I unpack it a little, more becomes clear.

When I remember the past few years and how my drinking has basically hijacked my life, I realize that I have gotten lost in it. Buried alive. I've lost the ability to be all things Sherry and now only feel confident in a social setting when armed with liquid courage. I can't remember the last time I attended an event completely sober. Whether a football game or a birthday party, I have become completely reliant on alcohol to get me through.

I ride the next few hours mulling all this over. In the past year some of my close friends have told me that they like me much better when I'm not drinking, but until now I didn't know what they meant. Without alcohol I assumed I was very blasé, without humor—really just not fun at all.

The glimpse of this realization brings me to tears. Happy tears. It gives me hope that maybe I can keep going into a sober life after the trip, something I'd put out of my mind. I am doing one day at a time right now, and it has nothing to do with AA and everything to do with physically getting through every day.

I feel wonderful this afternoon. We have a tailwind, no doggie surprises, and I just feel free! So free, in fact, that I moon the SAG vehicle when we pass it (I ensure I'm in the back of the line, of course). This is no small feat on a bicycle, and even though I would have previously thought I could only moon someone while inebriated, I discover I can also do it sober! In fact, in this case I probably couldn't have done it while drinking, as it takes a lot of balance to moon someone while riding a bike.

The last ten miles this afternoon are along this beautiful cedar swamp. It's so incredibly beautiful that we all spread out from our usual tightknit pack of bikes and just enjoy that last hour each on our own.

I ride with glistening eyes and a big smile. I'd unpacked a lot about myself this afternoon. I ride with my forbidden earbuds playing Chris Tomlin's rendition of "Amazing Grace," and it's so fitting that I press repeat for miles.

"My chains are gone . . .!" I feel those chains breaking with every stroke of the pedal. The chains of alcohol and the path of self-destruction it had led me down were being flung off me one after another. In my mind I have a visual that reminded me of the character Forrest Gump from the movie by the same name—you know, the scene when his braces fly off as he runs? Jenny is shouting "Run, Forrest, run!" I hear, "Ride, Sherry, ride!" I feel like I'm riding away from the grip of alcohol. Not running away anymore, but letting it go.

As I approach the SAG vehicle, I take one last look at the cedar swamp I've been riding next to these last ten miles, and I take a mental picture so I can pull out this beautiful emotion it has brought me to when I need strength—the strength to keep letting go.

Daily Rider Report—Day 7

We are really tired tonight, so this will be very short. We will post tomorrow again. We have arrived safely in Little Rock, Arkansas, after biking 102 miles. We then drove to Kirby, Arkansas, where we will spend the weekend.

We thank you for all your prayers, and we assure you that we will blog completely tomorrow. We will also try to get photos up so you can see all of this in living color. We'll close with our quote for the day: "You don't have to be crazy to do this, but it sure helps!"

(Report from the Riders, Ride4Life blog post, September 4, 2010, https://lpcride.blogspot.com/2010/09/report-from -riders.html.)

12

Happy Hours and Holidays

After my victorious and freeing Forrest Gump biking high, it's back to the reality of loading bikes, grabbing water, and settling in for the SAG ride to our destination for the night: the Self Creek Inn in Kirby, Arkansas. We're going to spend the next two days of Labor Day weekend relaxing there. I'm skeptical of our upcoming R&R weekend because I'd just survived an entire week of the seediest motels I've ever experienced. Granted, I hadn't experienced many until recently, but still.

I tell myself not to get too excited about this weekend's destination because the same guy who chose the motels also chose this lodge. And what kind of name is Self Creek anyway? I wonder if it will be rustic, like camping. It sounds like a good place to be all by myself, and I'm ready for a little space.

Knowing we have a few hours' drive ahead, I settle into the back seat of the van and shut my eyes, listening to the chatter around me. My ears are picking up talk from my teammates that they feel guilty taking a day off and want to ride "for the fun of it" tomorrow. I keep my eyes shut, but my brain is screaming "No freaking way!" I am off the blue bike for two days and intend to stay off.

৪৩৪৩৪৩

Craig and I had camped since the beginning of our marriage. Starting in a tent, we slowly upgraded to bigger and better campers by fixing them up and reselling them and then buying another fixer-upper, each one a little bigger and a little newer, until we ended up in a more permanent setting. In the summer of 2000 we made a big move from a permanent camping spot in Montague, Michigan, to a recreational camping park only twenty minutes from our home.

Don't get me wrong—we didn't want to leave the spot in Montague, but our park was sold to the county and would no longer allow seasonal camping. It was right on Lake Michigan, and we had been there for three summers, which consisted of sitting on the beach all day while our kids played in the waves, built dams, and climbed dunes.

Those were idyllic summers. I don't recall drinking during the day there, but I looked forward to those nightly campfires where the Captain Morgan and Diet Dr Pepper flowed freely. I'm sure I drank more than I should have, and I remember being a little impressed with my tolerance level.

On Sundays the guys would go home, and the girls would have more beach day on Monday before we headed home. Then we'd all head back to the campground on Thursday and do it all over again. The dads came back on Friday after work, and I loved hearing the kids (and there were a lot of them!) yell "The dads are here!"

I loved those years and wish I could have stayed right where I was. Nevertheless, in 2000, it ended and we needed to find a new place to spend our summers. I often wonder what would have happened had we stayed put.

I was dead set against moving our camping location to Sandy Pines, a "campground" about twenty minutes from our home on a small inland lake. Golf carts were the main mode of transportation. The tiny lake was so congested with boats that it was a death wish to take the kids tubing on the weekends.

My friend and camping buddy from Montague had grown up there, and she pushed us hard to take a look. So one night the four of us met a Realtor and rode around on her executive golf cart, checking everything out. My first complaint was that it was so woodsy! I was a sun girl all the way, and this place was a no-go in my head until the Realtor took us to see a new phase of the park. All the lots were on a small cove off the lake with few trees. Many lots were for sale where we could consider putting our trailer until we achieved our dream of upgrading to one of the park model trailers so popular there.

The park models were like little mobile homes. They were tricked out with screened rooms and decks for luxury summer living. To me, this looked like the way to go. Most of the trailers in this cove area were newer, well-kept park models except for one. That particular park model looked like it had been dumped on a lot and not cared for since. The weeds were taking over, it lacked landscaping, and the pretty walkways everyone else had were nowhere to be seen.

Craig asked the Realtor what was up with this sorry park model amid all the newer ones. When she replied, my adrenaline kicked in. "This one is going on the market tomorrow. It's a divorce special." My husband and I are the Chip and Jo of trailer fixer-uppers. We had bought and sold five to work our way to our current one. This trailer looked like the golden ticket to Sandy Pines. We bought it immediately and the work began, along with having a whole new place for me to drink.

Happy hours were abundant in this delightful new place. I started living there in the summer so my kids could have the experience of living in a neighborhood. Our home was in the country, and it was much easier to keep them occupied here than at home. So began the blissful summers at Sandy Pines.

So also began the period when my drinking was more frequent. I would drive through those gates and feel my body relax in anticipation of the glass of wine I would pour while I was unpacking. I always let my kids go play instead of helping unpack because I wanted to light a cigarette and enjoy my wine. I would leisurely unpack unless I was interrupted—or let myself be interrupted. If my neighbor girlfriends were hanging out on a deck nearby, I would grab my glass and the unpacking would be lost to laughing and drinking with the girls until the husbands started arriving. Those were good times, and I didn't see the trouble I was setting myself up for. It all seemed like innocent fun.

It was easy to drink there; I didn't have to drive, my kids were always occupied, and I basically had no responsibilities. Looking back, I was losing my family and chose to ignore it. My older daughter wasn't a fan of the Sandy Pines lifestyle, and as soon as she got her driver's license she got off the golf cart and was out and about as much as possible. My son truly loved it and spent every waking moment with his best friend, who lived next door. Fishing, golfing, tubing (pulled by a sober me), and flying around on the golf cart looking for girls. My younger daughter was with me a lot. She grew up at Sandy Pines, taking tennis lessons and going to kids' club. In later years she taught tennis and was a leader at kids' club, which gave me a lot of unsupervised time alone.

My drinking really escalated for the first nine years we were there, and then when the stop button was applied to me in 2010, I turned it into a hide button. Living there became a struggle, a push-pull between Craig and me until I grew to hate it. No privacy, watchful eyes, and a fire every night that I didn't want to sit by.

I didn't know how to do life sober at what was once my favorite place to be. Being there was too hard without drinking. I spent a lot of time isolating myself in that little park model, drinking alone and making sure I cleared out my stash of empties on trash day.

Then there was floating on inner tubes. I hated the stinky inland lake, but somehow I'd made it more tolerable by drinking. When I wasn't drinking I wanted nothing to do with it. But on the weekends my neighbors would all float together in front of our place on the cove. They'd be tied up together with coolers bobbing among them. I hated missing out, and there wasn't any way to escape it when I was there. Until I got my bike. I found so much freedom on my bike those summers I was training for the Ride4Life. I could go off on my bike for hours while they floated their summer away. I would feel healthy and strong only to return to the same scenario every time and fight the urge to go to the party store. Again.

Sandy Pines became a game of hide-and-seek. I stayed sober for two of the last three summers we were there. God had more plans for us. I was ready to leave but my youngest daughter was pissed. We'd promised her that we would stay until her high school graduation, but that was all.

ಬುಬುಬು

I was jolted from my restful funk of dozing and daydreaming by the crunch of tires on gravel. I braced myself to take a look at our surroundings, and lo and behold, I was pleasantly surprised. It was beautiful!

PART 5

RELIEVED

13

Hills and Valleys

I wake up cautiously each morning. I first try to remember which gross motel I'm in and in which town. This morning is different. Without even opening my eyes I can tell I'm in a marvelous, cushy bed. It feels amazing, and I slept like a rock. When I realize my roommate is up and gone, I get up and head to the kitchen. Smelling coffee, I walk to it like an insect drawn to light. I see all the other women are up and about. There they are, my people. It's just us in this part of the lodge. I've grown to love each and every team member during this past week, and I anticipate a relaxing morning around the coffeepot with them.

Conversation is difficult on our bikes. The wind makes it hard to hear, and we rarely can ride side by side, so we're usually having a shouted conversation. I haven't divulged too much personal information to anyone here, keeping things light. Hadn't felt the urge to shout, "Hey, does anyone else here drink too much?"

As I enter the kitchen the others start to laugh, obviously at me. Laugh *and* point at my head. I duck into the bathroom for a look and start to laugh with them. Let's just say I didn't even know my hair was capable of sticking up in those never-before-seen directions and heights. Yes, there are pictures.

After coffee and a huge breakfast, we agree to do a fifty-mile ride through the beautiful area we're in. I protest a little but know they're right. We feel that we owe it to the people who have pledged money, whom we have told we would be riding every day. (Note that I never said that). Also, taking two days off riding would allow for a lot of stiffness to settle in, so we decide that riding is a good idea for our bodies as well and I agree with that part wholeheartedly. I feel one hundred years old just sitting around all morning. My muscles are stiff and sore.

However, my biggest issue is my hands. They are constantly numb while I am riding, and a few times I've gotten scared about my ability to squeeze the brakes. At night they cramp up painfully, and I wake up to clenched fists that I cannot uncurl. I have to massage and manipulate my hands open before I can do anything. I'd asked for prayer but hadn't shared with anyone how bad they were really getting.

We set off for our extra miles around the countryside thinking they will be easy. We soon realize that this will be a challenging ride, not leisurely. These backroads are like roller coasters! We find ourselves constantly on a steep climb only to fly down the other side of the hill. On the first major downhill we encounter, I quickly realize I'm in trouble. I'm going downhill way faster than I'm comfortable doing, and my hands simply cannot hold the brakes—not even to slow me down a little. I begin panicking, trying to hold it together as I fly by the rest of the group. I know that something as little as a piece of stray gravel could result in a major crash.

I coast to a stop as the ribbon of the road starts another ascent. I tell the other riders to keep going, that I am fine, and I wait for the SAG vehicle to roll up next to me. The driver, my good friend Carolyn, sees that I'm not, in fact, fine. My knees start to shake as the fear and realization of what could have happened set in. I tell her what just occurred.

Carolyn shakes her head. "There's no way you can ride today. Your hands have to heal before you can ride again."

I feel defeated. I'd sworn I would never get off the bike and into the van unless the whole team had to. But I know Carolyn is right—it makes total sense—but that doesn't stop me from having a giant meltdown on the side of the road. We load my bike and catch up with the team to let them know I'm getting in the van. I offer no explanation except holding up my hands and shrugging my shoulders. I feel so much shame. I obviously have to heal, but I still beat myself up for it.

The other SAG vehicle stays with the riders, and Carolyn and I head to find a store for needed supplies—namely ice, and I of course would use the restroom, just because there was one. When I come out of the restroom I load up on my staples: purple Propel and a bag of Peanut M&M's. But at the counter I find myself staring at the cigarettes and liquor behind the clerk. I drop the candy as I decide to indulge in a different vice. "Cigarettes please, whatever you've got. Menthol is good. And a lighter."

When Carolyn comes out of the store laden with bags of ice, she starts to laugh (which is why I love her). Here I am, Miss Ride4Life herself in all her glory, sporting my ride jersey, and perched on the SAG vehicle's bumper smoking a cigarette. Carolyn is also amused by the creative way I figured out how to hold the cigarette since my hands, with the exception of my thumbs, are almost completely numb. I am determined; I find a way.

We set off to find the riders and hand out newly purchased Popsicles before they melt. When we catch up with the riders I go from being mad at my situation to grateful because the group's ride has turned into a four-legged nightmare.

We're in the backwoods of Arkansas. These dogs are used to roaming the roads without feeling threatened. I highly doubt they see many cyclists. The job of the SAG vehicle becomes running interference between the bikes and the dogs. I've never been so glad to not be on the road as I am today! I have a great afternoon riding in the passenger seat next to Carolyn and have a refreshing perspective on why things happen the way they do. To trust his plan and not my ego.

That night when we're ready for the meal that all hands helped prepare, we hold hands as Cliff leads us in prayer. Cliff, the guy who has become like a brother to me in a short period of time. He prays for each of us by name and speaks to God about what he loves about each of us. It is a beautiful expression of how close we've become. The prayer takes a while, and just as I'm wondering about the food getting cold, he prays for me.

"Lord, Sherry has become like a little sister to me. I love her humor and determination. She encourages all of us each day to laugh a little more and take life a little lighter." Cue the tears that seem to come easier and easier as I lower the walls of protection that keep me from feeling too much.

Cliff also asks for prayer for my hands from our prayer warriors back home, and when I go to bed that night my prayers are a conversation with God about trusting him. He has showed me again today that he knows best. I need to trust him with a lot more than potential dog chases. I pray that maybe he can help me with this whole new thing called sobriety I'm cautiously mulling over. Without the cushion of alcohol, my emotions are starting to expose themselves. While a little scary, it feels good to feel something other than the anger and shame that have been present in me for so long. I fall asleep feeling peaceful and cared for by my Father.

14

Holidays and Happy Hours

After a day of rest we leave our little refuge in the woods to complete the last two days of the ride. We're all anxious to get going and, surprisingly, antsy to get back on our bikes and into our usual routine. Knowing we have only two days left to get to our final stop is surreal to me.

My hands are healing and able to handle the brakes again. I feel amazing after a semi-restful weekend, and I can't recall when I've felt this good physically, mentally, and spiritually. *How do I take this feeling home with me?* The question makes me anxious to consider what to do when I get home. Drink? Not drink? I have no idea. Surely since I've been sober for the last ten days while doing something this difficult, I can do daily life at home without drinking too, right? I try to shake these thoughts off and am moderately successful as I remember how peaceful my time with God was last night. *Stay there. Stay there.*

The other issue heavy on my mind is that I can't go home and ask for help with this fresh start. I have to try this sober thing on my own *again*, and that hasn't worked well at all in the past. My family is under the impression that I haven't drank since the ruined Christmas party eight months ago. I won't even consider opening up that can of shame again. *However, I bet they have been suspicious a few times.*

The anxiety usually present when I worry if I've been found out is quickly replaced with an unhealthy smugness that I've managed to get away with something. *Hello, childish thought process.* I should have recognized this as a warning sign sooner—that I'm proud of getting away with drinking. As if vodka and I make a great team and if we have won once, we can win again! My alcoholic brain is a constant threat to me.

My longtime therapist taught me a self-assessment process: ask myself if what I'm experiencing or thinking is, in most cases, an adult thought or a childish thought. This one definitely falls in the childish category.

I haven't always taken the therapist's advice. I've been through a few of them over the years, totally wasting their time and mine as I did not reveal my drinking problem until a few years ago. My therapist recommended quitting drinking for one year. *Well, you'll have an almost two-week start when you get home. That leaves fifty weeks of abstinence.*

That thought is way too daunting, so I revert to AA sayings. I detest clichés, and AA is full of them. However, I must admit that they're good as long as I don't overanalyze them. Take the whole "one day at a time" thing. I can say to myself that "just for today" (another saying) I will not drink, but it's like, why bother? Because I *know* for a fact that I'm going to drink this weekend. Sure, I can say for the next fifty weeks that I am a sober queen, but it's not true because there is no way I am not drinking when we . . . I could insert just about any event or occasion into this thought process because I don't need much of a reason to drink. I can make pretty much anything a drinking event. Even if I'm the only one partaking.

My childish thoughts are interrupted as the shout goes up from the group that someone has blown a tire. The testosterone team goes to work, and I use the opportunity to check my phone.

Craig has texted me that the kids are out at the lake with him. It's Labor Day after all, which is definitely my least favorite day of the summer. It means packing up our little summer home for the winter and a ton of work to do when we get home. Unloading, laundry, and getting ready for school the next day on top of it. Add in a hangover, and I have all the key items for a disaster of a holiday. To say I am *not* homesick today is definitely an understatement. *Maybe they will do all the work for me.* Not likely, but it's a nice thought.

My thoughts instead go to what my family might actually be doing. Maybe the boys are enjoying a few beers while grilling. The girls are probably mixing up a summer cocktail while they prepare side dishes. This drinking scenario will continue through the meal, and then they'll grab their suits for an afternoon floating in the cove with the neighbors. They'll have coolers tied to the inner tubes and filled with icy beers, with a thermos of Sangria bobbing in the water. Craig will float with his buddies and be glad he doesn't have to worry about me sitting in the trailer alone, where I'd be pouting and plotting the fight I'd pick with him later because he's drinking and I can't.

By the time I get through this scenario in my mind, I'm pissed. How dare they enjoy themselves with alcohol while I'm gone! Knowing full well I can't partake, they're probably elated I'm off on this godforsaken bike almost a thousand miles away! *It isn't fair. They think I should quit drinking, but the minute I'm gone they're little party animals celebrating me being gone. I'm the one who repeatedly ruined the parties. They must be so relieved to have me out of their hair for almost two weeks.*

I know better than to let my thoughts wander that far. The truth is, the only reason there was ever alcohol at family gatherings was because I made sure it was available. After all, I could always justify my drinking if others joined me. Never mind that I was usually far ahead of anyone else when they took their first drink because I always pregamed in private so my drinking could appear to match the others'.

The other truth is that this scenario I created in my mind about my party-animal family does not exist. Since I had "quit drinking," I had apologized to my oldest children that there wasn't booze at the family gatherings. They were quick to assure me that they never wanted it in the first place. "Mom, you were the drink pusher," they said. "We can take it or leave it."

For an alcoholic, this makes no sense! I can't understand when people get up from their table in a restaurant and leave wine in their glass. I can't understand how people can exist with a full liquor cabinet and not have a nip every now and then throughout the day. I can't understand why all people who are "allowed to drink" aren't drinking all the time. Which is why I'm the alcoholic and the others fall into a different category altogether. I call them "Normies," and I don't understand them at all. Was I ever a Normie? Maybe?

The shout goes up that we're ready to roll again, and I delete the long and snarky text I'd composed for Craig, replacing it with a simple "Have fun." I stow my phone back in my bag and shove off. The destination today is Hugo, Oklahoma. Our first thirty miles are cool without much wind. Bliss! However, the day is heating up fast, and we want to keep our stops short and get off the road for the day as early as possible. That plan backfires about as much as Barb's bike tire, which blows two more times. It becomes obvious that she needs a new tire. But it's Labor Day and the likelihood of finding an open cycle shop is pretty slim. The guys patch the final tire blowout with a regular Band-Aid until we can get Barb a new tire. Miraculously it holds the entire day!

Later, after checking in to the motel (a definite downgrade from our weekend lodge accommodations), we head to a recommended burger joint known for its milkshakes. We love our ice cream! While we're eating, Betty's husband and daughter show up. They drove down to see us cross the finish line tomorrow, making this whole trip seem surreal—it's really coming to a close. Hugs all around and a bike tire for Barb, brought by Betty's family, make for a celebratory evening of food and fun. I go to bed full of excitement and apprehension. I'm probably the only one thinking this hard about what life will look like when we get home.

15

Tropical Storm Hermine

I wake on September 7, 2010, taking the first few moments—as I have the last ten mornings—to figure out where I am and why my body hurts everywhere. Then I remember. It's our last day. Today we ride into the convention center in Grapevine, Texas.

I lie there for a moment, wondering what it's going to feel like to wake up tomorrow and not have to ride my bike. I can't picture ever riding it voluntarily again. I'm excited to be done, but I'm also scared to leave the security bubble of the bike ride. A day on the bike doesn't hold any temptation to stop at the liquor store or engage in a constant mental argument over whether to drink. It's been virtually impossible to drink these last ten days, and my memories of the hangover I started this trip with are already distant but not forgotten. Why would I even *want* to go back to feeling that way ever again? In this moment I feel alive, genuine, and full of gratitude for this experience that just might forever change me.

A knock brings me back to reality. The ride isn't over yet; we still have a full day ahead. The knock is one of the guys. "I need your bike; we're loading up and hoping to drive out of the storm."

Are you kidding me? Many other times I'd longed for a legitimate break, a true excuse to not ride. Here it is on a silver platter on the last day of our ride. I'd hoped for this every other day but not now! Today I want to ride across the finish line doing the one-arm fist pump I hadn't dared to do when we left the starting line.

But we can't ride in this. It's not just raining; it's pouring down the kind of rain that falls in great sheets in a deafening deluge. I can hardly make out the motor home across the parking lot. We load up bikes, gear, and riders, and decide to drive for a little while to see if we can get ahead of the rain. It doesn't take long to figure out we're driving *into* the storm, not out of it.

We cross the line into Texas riding in the SAG vehicles and jump out for a picture by the "Welcome to Texas" sign, but we're all feeling let down. After the photo we stop at a McDonalds to talk about a new plan and, of course, eat massive amounts of fast food. Best meeting I've ever had!

There isn't a lot to decide. A tropical storm is in charge of our decisions, not us. We watch the TVs in McDonalds for a play-by-play of Tropical Storm Hermine, which had come in off the Gulf of Mexico and traveled through Texas and into Oklahoma as a tropical depression. Right across our path. Roads are flooding and wind speeds are around sixty miles per hour.

A part of me loves danger, emergency rooms, and tornado watches. But not today! Our situation is looking dire. We decide that we will ride just the last mile in the rain to the finish line. Sadly, it's our only option. To attempt riding anymore today is just not safe.

All the women load up into the van with Carolyn, and we have some reflective talk about the whole ride. Betty is penning a poem to share with us at our celebratory dinner tonight. I'm listening to a song on the radio that is grabbing my heart: "I'm Not Who I Was" by Brandon Heath.

Tears well up in my eyes as I think about the song's words. I am not who I was ten short days ago. This is where the miracle

I've been waiting for must be. I think of Craig and my kids. I wish more than ever that they could be at the finish line to see me. To really see me and realize that even though I'm an alcoholic, I'm not rotten to the core. Alcohol didn't make me a bad person. I can be a Christian and love God and be an addict. I just can't serve both God and my addiction, and maybe that's what this ride revealed. God loves me the same yesterday, today, and tomorrow, *but I can feel his presence more when I am sober.*

When we find a place to get on our bikes to ride into the convention center, the rain has slowed. Not stopped, but at least it's falling lighter. We're going to get wet, but we're here and we will finish this ride. The mood is quiet as we all organize ourselves into a line for that last mile.

I'm grateful for the rain. For the wetness it provides on my face to cover my tears. For the deafening sound it makes, masking my occasional sob. The weighty significance of it all as we ride that last mile is overwhelming. I have no idea what everyone else is going through, but I'm an emotional mess. I can't believe I did this ride. I'm so grateful for the experience and the environment of Christian fellowship I've enjoyed the entire time. I recall every day and how I saw God's powerful hand of grace and protection lead us into this moment of victory. I feel like I'm somehow perched above the group and watching us ride in. I'm not the only one with quiet tears of joy as we enter the tunnel of cheers and yells of "Way to go!" That one-arm fist pump? Nailed it.

PART 6

CONFUSED

16

Travel Plans

Just like that, Ride4Life is over. I did it, and I did it well, and now I can cross it off the bucket list it had never been on in the first place.

After a victory dinner at the Cheesecake Factory and eating—of course—cheesecake *and* everything else on the menu, we say our goodbyes. It feels sort of anticlimactic, like there should be so much more surrounding the end of this epic adventure.

I'll miss every one of my teammates; we have a special bond. We signed up for this craziness, and we did it, and only this group surrounding me knows what it took. No one at home will understand what we're feeling right now as we say our goodbyes.

I have no idea how to convey these feelings to Craig or anyone else. When friends had texted me about how the ride was going, I always talked about the hard bike seat and the effect it was having on my bottom half. To be truthful, my butt, and everyone else's, had been the least of our problems. Wind, rain, heat, breakdowns, and four-legged beasts had been much bigger concerns that weren't even on my radar before we left.

But instead of questions about all that, I desperately need someone to ask me today how I feel about staying sober tomorrow. I *need* to talk about this, but my fears of how it will be received are bigger than my need and, once again, I keep it to myself.

Tonight as we pack up and I lay out my outfit for the trip home, it feels unnatural. I'm used to laying out butt cream and bike shorts! I feel a little burst of pride as I set my alarm for the morning and realize I've allowed myself just thirty minutes to get ready and out the door. This is definitely an improvement as far as time management! An improvement Craig will appreciate. Pre-ride Sherry would require at least an hour to get ready, but alas, I'm a changed woman. From all outside appearances I'm ready. A teammate and I have an early flight and will be home by noon tomorrow. My bike and some of the team will be departing in the van tomorrow to drive back to Michigan.

Early in the morning I walk into the airport and see it like a mecca in the desert: *Starbucks*! I force myself to go through the check-in process first and then, on the other side of security, I finally hold the familiar cup in my hands. The coffee feels like liquid gold sliding down my throat.

We land in Grand Rapids and my husband is waiting for me. Emotions tumble through me when I see him. Gratitude, excitement, and most of all love. This guy is my rock. In this moment, as he gives me a bear hug, he whispers in my ear. "I am so, so, so very proud of you."

"Thanks," I say. "It is so, so, so good to be home."

Taking my hand firmly in his, Craig brings my fingers to his lips and kisses them as we walk out to his truck—where he gives me another hug as he holds the passenger door open for me. I feel his relief that I'm home safely. It's been a stressful couple weeks for him too. He's had to rely on text updates from me letting him know I'm safe.

"The best part of my day was always when I got your text saying 'off' and I knew you were done riding for the day. Then I could relax."

On the way home from the airport, we detour to see our son. Loren is mowing the lawn at one of our job sites. When he sees us approaching, he stops the mower and runs to the truck, giving me a huge hug as I get out. "Way to go, *Mom*! You did it! Was it awful?"

I laugh. "Thanks. I won't be doing it again anytime soon—or at all!"

We catch up for a few minutes and then Craig and I head home.

After unloading my stuff, Craig leaves me to unpack and, he assumes, to get some rest. He walks out the door, and so do I about five minutes later. I feel like an alien has attacked my brain. I don't take even a moment to list pros and cons or phone a friend to talk it out. No, I just readily give in to the impulse without one rational thought of the consequences to follow, falling hard, right back into the familiar pattern of day drinking. After driving to the closest liquor store and buying a fifth of vodka, I proceed to drink the afternoon away, pass out, and sleep until about 8 p.m. I lose about seven hours of the day.

When I come downstairs Craig and Olivia are chilling in the basement and had left dinner out for me. *Nice.* Instead of appreciating the effort, my alcoholic brain's way of thinking dominated. *They do just fine without me.* Clearly I'm not needed here. I feel like a stranger in my own home. As I look around, I notice the house is clean and picked up—Craig has even done my laundry. The mail is organized, and the dishes are done. Is he on to me or is he just being nice?

Craig shouts up the stairs. "Is the biker awake?"

"Yeah, be right down." I quickly dip a spoon in the peanut butter to mask any scent of alcohol lingering on my breath and go downstairs. Settling in next to Olivia, I catch up with her. In spite of the displaced feeling moments ago, it starts to feel good to be physically comfortable and in my home with my feet on the coffee table. Of course, my lingering buzz is helping to mellow my mood. I chat with them, and when their attention drifts back to the TV, I decide it's an appropriate time to gracefully duck out of family life. Feigning weariness, I say my good nights.

Back upstairs in the safety of my closet, I finish up the fifth and go back to bed. I pass out until the predictable three a.m. wake-up call. I hadn't missed this unwelcome alarm that my brain sets whenever I drink. Here I am, wide awake with a racing mind full of anxious thoughts. I don't know why this always happens when I drink, but the only way to get back to sleep is to drink more. Big problem though: I don't have any alcohol left. Not even in any of my emergency stashes in various shoe boxes and the other places I usually hide it. I'd done a sweep before I left on the ride so there wouldn't be any in the house to tempt me when I got home. Seemed like a good idea at the time.

I lie there and talk to God for a few minutes. He doesn't feel like the same God who was with me throughout the ride. He must be very disappointed in me. I turned my back so quickly on everything he taught me these last two weeks. He hadn't rescued me from drinking as I'd hoped. Of course, there's this thing you're supposed to do before you go do the wrong thing, that thing called *prayer*. It wasn't God who turned away; it was me. All me. I'm back in my world, the world I don't know how to be sober in. The world where it's easier to turn my back on God instead of seek him.

I had prayed this bike ride would relieve me of the constant drama I play like a recording in my head. Questions I just can't answer. *Why did I drink again? Why can't I stop? What's wrong with me?* I had spent hours thinking about this on the ride, and in a few short minutes I'm right back where I started. I have a starring role in the sitcom I call *Sherry Drinks Too Much*, starring Sherry, because it's all about Sherry! Today's episode is called "Drinking Games." It's Sherry versus the booze, and there can only be one winner. Did the Ride4Life cure Sherry of her addiction? Will she drink again? Will Craig kick her to the curb? Stay tuned!

This is how I feel. Like I'm sitting above my life watching it play out in TV episodes. Sitting cross-legged, floating in the air with my chin in my hands. Shaking my head at the choices I make. Sometimes yelling "Don't do it!" and "Why are you ignoring me?" Sherry doesn't listen to the voice of reason. The drinking voice is drowning it out. The one that says, "Go ahead, you deserve it." "It's not going to hurt anything." "You'll quit tomorrow."

Would I though? Quit tomorrow?

I drift back into a fitful sleep and pretend to be in a deep sleep when Craig leans in for a kiss goodbye. "Don't feel like you have to do a ton today," he says. "I think I'm pretty much caught up around here for you."

Yeah, I know. Getting Olivia off to school will be my biggest responsibility. The day stretches ahead full of choices to make. Plans to fail or plans to succeed. It reminds me of a familiar verse, Jeremiah 29:11: "'For I know the plans I have for you,' says the LORD, 'They are plans for good and not for disaster, to give you a future and a hope'" (NLT).

I ponder this verse. In my heart I know God wants me to succeed. I just have to get on board and trust his plan. I feel like he's failed me so many times—what could possibly be different about today? There lies a big part of my problem. It's easier to blame God for my failed plans instead of taking responsibility for myself.

Round Two

The Ride4Life is old news. I am a has-been. Surprisingly, I still seek solace on my bike. "Doing a thirty" (riding thirty miles) on a pretty fall day is now a pleasure. I can choose the route (clear of dogs) and set out with favorable temperatures and wind direction. I also want to lose weight. I'm very upset that I *gained* weight on the ride instead of losing it because apparently it *is* possible to eat more calories than I burned. It seems very unfair that I can burn five thousand calories in a day and come home bigger than when I left.

A big part of my thoughts every day is consumed with dieting. I resolve each morning how much I'll burn exercising and what I will or will not eat. My day looks like a fat camp rule book. If I do this I'll be able to better stick to my resolve when the late-day drinking thoughts begin to take hold. I don't always win this battle, but the drinking episodes are not as frequent as in the past.

This change isn't because I'm slowly healing, going to meetings, journaling, and talking to God. No, I'm trying out a man-made earthly strength named Antabuse. It's a prescription drug used to treat chronic alcoholism. There's a medical explanation for how this drug works, but the short version is that if you drink while it's in your system, you'll experience rather unpleasant side effects.

Round Two

Taking this medication and still drinking requires strategic planning. My plan is to take this pill each morning in front of Craig. He sets off for the day relaxed, knowing that the pill will keep me from drinking. Happy for him, I guess, but I'm smarter than that. If I know he's going to be out of town I stop swallowing the pill at least three days beforehand.

I'd read on a website that I shouldn't drink within twenty-four hours of taking Antabuse. I tested the waters a few times and know the waiting period for me is at least forty-eight hours. If I try to drink too soon after ingesting the Antabuse, my body goes into a feverish frenzy. Every bit of me turns bright red, even the whites of my eyes. My heart will pound. It's scary and very uncomfortable. The few times I drank too early I ended up hiding in bed to wait it out.

After a while Craig quits supervising me, assuming that I still take the pill on my own. But I quit taking it altogether, at least not every day. It's much easier to keep my drinking options open without Antabuse's interference. I still occasionally take it on my own, mostly on Sunday through Wednesday. This goes hand in hand with my dieting habits.

Each week has the same pattern: super restrictive starting on Monday and breaking all my rules by Thursday. I'd drink and let my guard down against food, and then sugar beware—there isn't a morsel of junk food in the house that is off-limits.

I journal every day, and my writings are basically about what I need to do to lose weight, quit drinking. and spend less, as spending money is still a problem too. However, life isn't all bad, and I think I've found somewhat of a balance with my drinking.

My drinking rules are as follows:

1. *Drink alone and never before an event or gathering.* The weekends that Craig will be gone are the perfect time to drink alone. Party of one all weekend.

2. *Say no to invitations from friends so I can stay home, drink, pass out, and repeat.* Then on Sunday shakily pick up the house and

95

make myself presentable. Also possibly haul out a project to make it look like I've been occupied all weekend while Craig was gone. Rehearse my lines about what I've done over the weekend and hide any evidence of alcohol. Resolve to never do this to myself again, and start out with the usual strong resolve and determination that Mondays bring.

ೞೞೞ

I go back to work part-time at the pregnancy center, and I have incredible days of personal victory there, days I'm able to pour into prospective volunteers and be part of strategic planning for the future. God is so present in this place, and I feel so alive when I'm here working. I'm even training to teach the curriculum for the volunteer training.

Currently I work on Mondays and Wednesdays, and these days are when I'm my best self. Instead of offering to volunteer on the other days that were hard for me, instead of asking for help from the few people I'm close to, I didn't say anything. I'm just too proud and don't want to damage the image I've built at work. I've built an image of self-confidence mixed in with a flashy style and a cocky attitude. It's like a command performance every week, and I love to perform. My friend Carolyn at the center knows my struggles, but I'm always quick to assure her that I'm doing great, and careful not to give her reason to worry or ask questions.

On my drive home from work I pass a few of my most-frequented liquor stores and toss around the idea of stopping in my mind for a minute. Then relief washes over me because I can't drink. I've taken Antabuse and drinking isn't an option today. You'd think that feeling of relief would be enough to keep me going on the sober trail, but I'm always easily swayed as the weekend approaches.

Spring 2011

I hear rumors about the next Ride4Life going to Orlando. It takes me a while to warm up to the idea of participating again. I've compared the Ride4Life to childbirth many times; it's ironic that this is a charity ride for a pregnancy center.

The Similarities Between Childbirth and Ride4Life

Childbirth: It takes about nine months to get to the big day, and no matter how much you try, nothing can fully prepare you for how hard it will be. When you are in the middle of labor, it hurts like hell and seems never-ending and you say never ever again. But then you finally hold that precious, beautiful baby in your arms.

A year or two later you find yourself pregnant again, even though you'd said never ever again, and when that first contraction hits it all comes rushing back. *Nooo! How did I let myself get into this predicament again?*

Ride4Life: You spend months in nervous anticipation, wondering if you're training enough to be ready. You say your goodbyes and ride off with the group while consumed with worry about the challenge ahead. You say to yourself never ever again every single day, and then you cross the finish line and the victory is oh so sweet. Still, you say never ever again.

Time passes. Winter is long, and you yearn to be outside in the sun riding your bike. The Ride4Life 2011 approaches and your brain says, "You know, it wasn't so bad." And you find yourself biking from Michigan to Orlando with your brain (and everything from the waist down) screaming in protest: "You said we weren't doing this again!"

Here I am considering the ride because the brain has the ability to dull the intensity of past experiences. I say yes. This time, though, I'll have a little more control and hopefully a little more fun. I also hope that this ride will work in my favor and I'll be freed from my addiction.

First item in my preparations is recruiting an innocent friend. I choose Bonnie. She's a volunteer at the pregnancy center, and we'd made an instant connection at the volunteer party last Christmas. This isn't exactly spiritual (that comes later), but we first admired each other's sense of style. Shoes and clothing will draw two women close faster than the spoken word any day.

Bonnie had mentioned a few times that she was thinking about doing the Ride4Life, and one day she told me she'd bought a road bike to start training. Yes! A friend on the ride who enjoys my stories, provides good conversation, and—most importantly—shares my fashion sense! Yes, fashion sense; Bonnie is the first one to wear biking apparel in a leopard print. To say I'm jealous is an understatement.

Bonnie knows nothing of my constant conundrum surrounding drinking, and I have no intention of sharing it with her. Why would I, when I have every intention of getting it under control? I will bury it so deep that there isn't any chance of it resurfacing. I'm sure that sounds a little skewed, but if you're trying to get rid of a drinking problem like I am, you get it. You don't know how to fix it. You just want it to go away so you can resume life—a life that includes "normal" drinking.

So I decide to ride again, and I set off for Orlando with more confidence than I had a year ago. This time Carolyn is our chief SAG driver, which means many things. The most important is that break stop snacks and meals will no longer be served on a beach towel. Derek is also back, now serving as our ride leader for the entire trip. In total, eight riders and five SAG assistants push off from the same parking lot we had a year ago, with friends and family cheering us on as we ride out. I give a one-armed wave without a second thought; I'd practiced making it look natural. So here I am, sailing along feeling a little puffed up and proud, when only one mile later we have our first collision. A teammate falls directly over her handlebars and takes a nasty spill.

Thank God she is OK, but it puts us in a somber mood for those first fifteen miles. Danger is everywhere and can pop up out of nowhere. We have to pay attention every moment. Staying focused on my front tire and the back tire of the bike in front of me is, I think, where some of the mental exhaustion comes in. We can't let our guard down for a second.

With everyone quiet and in their own thoughts for this first leg, I let my thoughts wander. The more I think about it, I'm a little amazed at the correlation between biking and drinking. In both situations I have to be on guard at all times. One stray thought about imbibing and I am driving to the liquor store five minutes later. On the bike you are one wandering thought away from a crash when you take your eyes off the tire of the person in front of you. This has been my constant battle.

My impulses scare me because they come out of nowhere sometimes. I'll think I'm in the clear for the day, and in a split second I'm spiraling into a bender. A verse from 1 Peter comes to mind, and I feel it was written with me in mind. "Be sober-minded; be watchful. Your adversary the devil prowls around like a roaring lion, seeking someone to devour" (1 Peter 5:8 ESV).

That's why Antabuse, when I use it as intended and am committed to sobriety, is a huge aid. At times the cravings have been so strong that I try drinking anyway and that doesn't turn out well. Other times I am flat on my face sobbing because I want to give in to the impulse and can't. That's Antabuse doing its job well.

One difference in this Ride4Life is I'm starting it hangover-free. Well, almost. I quit drinking a few days ago. OK, yesterday was my first alcohol-free day so today is technically day two.

It took everything in me not to drink yesterday. I felt awful, and the temptation to fix the problem with the same problem almost won out. But I pushed through. Not wanting a repeat performance in the gas station bathroom at our first stop is one of the many reasons I refrained yesterday. I'm not that strong, though, and a bad memory hasn't ever stopped me before. If that worked I could pull out a bad memory every time I'm tempted and have sweet success in sobriety every day. The truth is, I took Antabuse.

I hope this trip will be different from my first Ride4Life. It's kind of surreal biking to Florida, a state I've been to many times as a kid on road trips. The drive took forever in a car, so to go there on a bicycle seems like a big deal. Plus, when we start out, the weather conditions in Michigan are cool and fall-like. When we reach Florida, we have a few days with temperatures in the upper 90s, even edging above 100 degrees.

This time when we bike to the finish line at the Care Net Conference in Orlando we're ecstatic—only to arrive to a very small group of people waiting for us. I actually wonder if we are in the right place. Turns out we are, but there just wasn't as much hype around the ride this year.

We're invited to come into the convention center with our bikes and join the chairwoman on stage as she announces our arrival. This sounds more like it! Much to our disappointment, said stage was just a small, square platform in the middle of a trade-show atmosphere. No one pays attention as she interviews Derek about our journey. We leave and go outside for our own celebration. We take tons of pictures together, and my favorite is one in which I'm lifting my bike over my head in victory. We have the second annual celebratory dinner that evening, and the next morning I fly home. From there it's a repeat of last year's ending, right down to the part where I head to the liquor store as soon as Craig leaves.

18

Insanity

Insanity (noun): Doing the same thing over and over while expecting different results.

I'm a master at wrecking the work. A prime example is the Ride4Life that I've now completed twice. I train all summer to participate. I get so close to my God. I'm encouraged both by my ability to do hard things and by the fellowship of good Christian teammates. I return home equipped and empowered to continue on the path of sobriety. Then I wreck the work. I drink and continue boarding the roller coaster of my drinking life that I've been riding for so many years.

The first time I heard the definition of insanity (in AA, of course), I could totally relate. Now I see a shift. I no longer expect different results. Each time I drink it's always the same: I drink too much, pass out, and promise I won't drink again.

My journals are full of day-one declarations of this is "my last day one ever!" I write this phrase so often I no longer believe it, resulting in absolutely no faith in myself or and my ability to completely quit. I feel sadly resigned to this secret life of drinking, and this is where I stay for the next few months of 2011.

I have the best of intentions every day. I always feel close to God in the morning in my prayers, as I plead with him to keep me sober today. I journal everything I hear from him and what he puts in front of me in scripture or wisdom from someone else. Then I walk away, and I seemingly forget everything he's shared with me as the day goes on. My biggest problem is my black-and-white thinking: if one thing goes wrong, the whole day is messed up and, behold, that's a reason to start drinking. Drinking then leads to overeating, and I let myself be lax in my food choices. Then the next morning I wake up with the infamous empty pit that only carbs can fill. Feeling tired and hungover definitely does not lead to exercise, and I'm now in a three-way destructive hurricane that will catch me in its eye for at least a few days, though most often it's more like a week. Just like the storm, there will be cleanup in the aftermath. Mostly in my relationship with Craig.

I read somewhere that the power of sin within me keeps sabotaging my best intentions, and that is the only explanation I can come up with when I try to analyze why I keep drinking. Thank goodness God isn't done working with me, no matter how often I try to wreck the work.

ജ്ഞ

February 2012

I'm terrified of the travel I'm about to embark on. Olivia is singing in Disney World with her high school choir and my older daughter, Abby, and I are going to go see her perform and hang out (just the two of us) in Florida for a few days. Abby and I have not vacationed alone before, and to be truthful, we haven't desired to. We've had a tumultuous ten years. All those awful things you hear about teenage girls and their mothers? That's us. On steroids. We're as far from a Hallmark movie as you could possibly get. More like a Lifetime original called *My Daughter Is Evil* and if she picks the title, I'm sure it'll be something like *My Mother Is a Psychopath*.

When she went off to college, things settled down a little, and even more so when she got married three years ago, but we still walk on eggshells around each other. Neither one of us *wants* to fight, but arguments can come out of nowhere. The truth is, even though neither one of us will ever admit it, we're alike. Explosive, reactive, argumentative, and sensitive to the core. The thought of enjoying a few days traveling together? It's a mystery to both of us how this will play out. All that aside, I invited her to join me (dang impulses) while honestly not thinking she would say yes, and I think she surprised herself when she said yes.

So here we are about to get on a plane together. To add to this drama, I'm eight days sober with absolutely no intention of drinking while I'm with her. She is way too smart for me to even think about trying. Here's the thing: when push comes to shove, I can do this sober thing.

The days pass and we have an amazing time together. It truly is the start of a change in our relationship. One night she asks me the question I've always feared being asked by my children.

"Mom, did I make you drink?" The look on Abby's face is guarded but also vulnerable.

I respond 100 percent honestly. "No one person or thing can ever make me drink. That choice has always been my own."

Later I reflect on my carefully rehearsed answer and I know in my heart that it's true. I like to blame so many people and things in my life for my out-of-control drinking, but I cannot use them as a reason to stay in this bondage. Abby's question forces me to take a good hard look at my drinking and how much I blame everything and everyone for my addiction.

I draw the biggest strength to stay sober during this trip from not wanting to hurt her. I don't want to wreck the work. We've worked on our relationship over the past few years, and the thought of drinking while on our girls' weekend never even occurs to me. So sober I stay. That trip becomes a game-changer in our relationship, and my takeaway will always be what I learned in those four short days. If I can stay sober when it's absolutely necessary, maybe, just maybe, being sober is where true change and healing will happen.

Winter moves into a spring of contemplation of making a real change. I've been stringing together quite a few days of sobriety. It's excruciatingly difficult and tiring work. The times that I break my sober streaks come down to a few stupid reasons why I cave to the bottle.

- The opportunity is there—meaning I've forgotten to take my Antabuse and then forgot it on purpose for a few days in case I decide to drink.
- I lose my focus and turn my attention to diet woes or my job, or I pile too many things on my plate instead of paying attention to the triggers that lead me to drinking.
- I sacrifice my morning quiet time with God in the name of exercise, always with an intent to do both, but instead I'm running late for work and skipping God-time altogether.
- I drink once after thirty days sober to celebrate my longest sober run yet.

When I do the work it takes to stay sober, it affects how I think about drinking. I'm learning how to recognize the warning signs of an impending binge and take preventative measures. I recognize that I must stop the roaring train of drink-craving before it derails completely and I'm in the liquor store parking lot. So I make a few things nonnegotiable. If I follow the rules, it's much easier and far less dramatic to stay sober.

- A quiet time of meditation with God in the morning is a must. I write down on index cards the things that really speak to me in my quiet time and keep them near me throughout the day. Whether it's a verse or words of wisdom from a devotional, those cards are in my car, on the kitchen windowsill, and wherever else I might be that day.

- I have a schedule with no room for a wandering mind. I schedule everything from appointments, to cleaning the bathrooms, riding my bike, and phoning a friend. A scheduled day for this busy mind of mine is a game-changer to stay sober.
- Prayer is also a scheduled task. I write out prayers to say during challenging times. For instance, three a.m. has its own prayer: "Lord, I just want to check out now. Help me to keep on the path and not stray."
- I ride my bike, especially if the sun is shining. Or I plan to go for a ride after dinner and then all I have to do is shower, stay out of the kitchen, and get to bed with a good book. I tell my husband that it's nothing personal that I'm not hanging out on the comfy couch, but I just need to be where I feel safe. This is always my bed.

On June 13, 2012, I make a commitment to a sober summer. We're getting ready to move to the lake for the rest of the summer and Sandy Pines is a huge part of my demise into alcoholism. I know I can't blame the physical place; more to blame is the leniency I gave myself when drinking there. I drank in secret the last two summers. I long to be outside at night, around the campfire with a drink in my hand. To do so without a drink is unthinkable.

At times I drank to oblivion inside my trailer while everyone else was outside around the fire. On a few occasions I went out and entertained them with the drunken Sherry show for all to see when my liquid courage told me to go outside and play. This year will be different. I'm committing to a sober summer. I'm not allowing myself to think ahead any further than that. One season at a time is the best I can manage.

Journal Entry

My training for the Ride4Life 2012 is on fire! I am not smoking or drinking, and I am eating like a health nut. Who am I?! The better I feel, the more empowered I am becoming. I can feel myself being restored physically, emotionally, and spiritually. Why on earth would I ever go back to a life of drinking, hangovers, and hiding? When it came time to move home on Labor Day, the tears poured down my cheeks as I drove out of the gates. I had done it and, in this moment, I have no desire to drink now that the summer is over. Thank you, God, thank you.

PART 7

YIELDED

19

More Than One Kind of Stormy Weather

The summer of 2012 is one of the hottest on record in Michigan. This summer we remodel our kitchen, our basement floods (adding to the remodeling project), and our dog dies. I could write a country music song about this frenzied summer, except most of those musings end with "Pour Me Another" after the dog dies. I do not, however, pour anything.

The final days of preparation for the Ride4Life 2012 are underway, and I'm not drinking at all. I need to stay on top of my game right now. I am Sherry, the Ride4Life leader this year! Me, the girl who didn't even know what the word *drafting* meant (riding close behind another rider so they block the wind for you) now calls myself a roadie (the nickname for a dedicated road cyclist). I am teaching a few young women who have signed up for the ride this year to "speak bike," and one of them is my son's high school sweetheart, Stephanie.

Seemingly out of nowhere Stephanie and I had a conversation one night, and she asked me if I thought she could do the ride. A couple of young women she knew had expressed interest, and I had secretly been wishing she was one of them.

"Do you think I could do Ride4Life?" she asked.

My reply was immediate: "If I can, anyone can."

She contemplated my answer for a moment with a furrowed brow. "I don't even own a bike."

"What's your point?" I said with a laugh. "Neither did I, and that can be easily taken care of."

"Well," she said slowly, "maybe we could just go look at them."

In that moment I knew I would be adding another rider. It's impossible to go to the bike shop and not get caught up in the impressive gadgetry of all things bike hanging from the ceiling. By the end of the following week, our Stephanie had a sweet white road bike and was starting to train.

We have young and old going on this year's trip, which is around Michigan. I'm really excited: so far we have young adults, a couple on a tandem, and a grandmother and her granddaughter who hold the titles of oldest and youngest team members. Add in the few returning bikers, and we have ourselves a team!

Our team leaves on a radiant September morning. It's a gorgeous Indian summer day. That weather extends into the next day, but that's where the run of good weather ends. Over the next week we rarely feel the warmth of the sun. Ride4Life 2012 is forever known as the ride with the worst imaginable Michigan weather. The warm sun gives way to a pelting cold rain that turns to sleet when the temps begin to fall into the forties.

During the part of the ride we had looked forward to the most, racing down one of the steepest roads in Michigan, we have to stop and take shelter in the woods while it hails mercilessly, making downhill conditions perilous for road bikers. The winds are also a fight for most of the ride. The bone-chilling cold in my feet and hands make every mile extra challenging. But this team is full of fight. And my future daughter-in-law? She's amazing, and everyone on the team loves her. You never hear her complain, and she always has this forced, brave smile on her face. I keep a close eye on her because if anything happens to her, I'll answer to my son, and he has made it clear that Stephanie is the love of his life.

When we ride across the finish line to the cheers of our loved ones on September 24, 2012, it's an incredible victory for all of us. This time our finish line is seventy-five loved ones lining both sides of the road. My tears sting my eyes and blur my vision. I'm crying so hard, and I've never been so happy for something to end as I am this ride. It's been hell. The day we ride in is my 103rd day of sobriety. I know without a doubt that there will not be a day 104.

I'll drink today. I've been telling myself these last few days that I deserve it. I'm not in a positive state of mind at all; I'm negative and angry about the miserable week we just endured and turn my back on seeing the light of protection God gave us through the ride, I'm blind to the relationships that formed into lifelong friendships, oblivious to the real victories: the funds raised and my leading this team to a safe return.

No, I was bitter, angry, and didn't need to look far for an excuse to drink. One hundred and three days was long enough. I deserved a drink, and another, and another. I spend a week binge drinking, trying to stop the voices in my head that are telling me what a failure I am. I'm a fake. Other people see a leader and I see only a loser. The more I beat myself up about who I'm not, the more I fight to drown the voices saying I'm not good enough.

I'm jolted out of my selfish week of binge drinking when my mom calls. It's early and she's abrupt. "Sherry, can I come over?"

I say yes hesitantly. I'm afraid my mom knows about my drinking and is going to call me out on it. Paranoia sets in and I wonder if someone tipped her off. *Who would do that? Maybe she spotted me coming out of a liquor store?* I have no idea why she's coming over, but about three minutes later she enters and within seconds we're on the floor as I hold her while she sobs.

"Mom, Mom, tell me." I start to cry myself. I know that whatever is happening is a brutal blow. This is a life-changing, horrific moment that alters your life's trajectory. Whatever it is has brought my mom to her knees. In sobbing gulps, she gives me bits and pieces.

Didn't want to tell you.

Didn't want you to think about it on the ride and be distracted.

The tests weren't good.

The cancer has spread.

Kidney failure.

Late-stage.

Chemo.

All the phrases that you dread hearing about someone you love. My mom is letting them out one by one is short bursts of excruciating pain. Through her agonizing sobs I slowly understand. There is only one person that the threat of losing could cause her to feel this horrific. Bob, my stepdad and my mom's husband of twenty-seven years, has cancer.

My mom and Bob are best friends. They do life as a team, always. They are *that* couple who don't need a large circle of people because they have each other and that's always been enough. Their song is Kenny Rogers's "Lady," and that's what Bob called her. They built two businesses around their shared passion of antiques and food, and I'd worked in both of them from the beginning. The businesses had started out with just the three of us and grown steadily over the years. I get along with Bob fairly well. We have had our moments over the years, but the quality I admire most about him is how much he adores my mom.

As I hold my mom, my mind goes to another time and place when my mom had been blindsided by the searing pain of losing a loved one. That time had been without warning, and there was no way she would have survived without Bob to hold her while she sobbed from the searing pain of losing a child. My little brother.

20

The Alcohol Effect

First you take a drink, then the drink takes a drink, then the
drink takes you.
—F. Scott Fitzgerald, *The Great Gatsby*

October 8, 1994

We were all up early on that Saturday morning, contrary to our
usual routine of sleeping in, watching cartoons, and eating a
leisurely breakfast. We were having family pictures taken and
were caught up in the calamity that brings, especially when
small children are involved.

Even though there were only the four of us, looking back
that morning reminds me of the scene in the movie *Home
Alone* when the family is all trying to get ready at the same
time and seemingly running in circles. Except in the movie
there are about twenty people! I recall the phone ringing in
the background and bits of the conversation my husband was
having.

"Who was that?" I asked while trying to get a spot off the
shirt my son needed to wear. The pieces that I had overheard
were enough to make me ask questions.

My husband's brow was furrowed, and his jaw was set as he
looked past me and not at me. He named a coworker of his.
"No worries. There was an accident near Steve's house. He

knew Steve was your brother and wanted to know if he was involved. We would've heard something if he was."

The phone rang again and my heart jumped. I was sure that we were getting bad news about that accident. I was quickly reassured when my husband mouthed "my mom." My in-laws lived on a dairy farm nearby and urgently needed Craig's help with a calf stuck under a fence.

"Go and come back as quick as you can," I said as I turned on the shower to start getting ready. It didn't take me long to forget about the first call about the potential accident. I found out later that Craig sensed that something was very wrong, and he took the phone off the hook when I got in the shower. He left feeling uneasy and didn't want the phone to ring while he was gone.

In the days of landlines, when you took the phone off the hook, a beeping sound occurred and then it went into a continuous buzzing. As I was getting ready, I heard that faint buzzing and put the phone back on the hook, thinking it must have come off in all the rushing around. I started to get ready, and that is when—through our second-floor bedroom dormer—I saw movement that would begin my descent into indescribable pain.

I was getting dressed when I noticed a white police car slowing down in front of our home. As if in a trance, I walked into the hallway and looked out the dormer window from above to see it turning into our driveway. By the time I got downstairs, it had slowly snaked up our long driveway and parked.

My heart was beating out of my chest. When I saw my stepdad get out of the car, I knew something was very wrong, and the only thing I could think of was that something happened to my mother. Bob would not leave her in her grief if it were a tragedy concerning anyone else. I flung the door open and demanded, "*What? What?* Tell me what's happened!"

My best friend's father was the police officer accompanying my stepdad, and he attempted numerous times to tell me the story, even with my many interruptions of "Just tell me!" The words slammed into my brain in little fragments: "There's been an accident . . . the vehicle rolled . . . Steve and his best friend . . . no survivors." The story concluded with the heartrending truth that my little brother was dead.

In a daze I told the officer where Craig was, and the officer called the farm at the same moment my husband was pulling into their driveway. Craig's mother came out of the barn, and by the look on her face, he knew he had to get back home. Without a word he backed out of the driveway and knew the suspicions he had tried to protect me from were true.

While we waited for Craig's return, I frantically tried to protect my five-year-old and seven-year-old from what was happening. Bob gently put his hands on my shoulders and said, "I've got them. Go get dressed. Your mom needs you."

Knowing that Bob wanted to get back to my Mom, I managed to call Craig's brother to come stay with the kids and then finished dressing. But when Craig walked into the bedroom, we collapsed into a puddle of grief onto the floor. After his brother arrived, we drove the mile to my mom's house. All I could think about was her pain. I too had a son, and to lose either of my children was such a horrific thought that I couldn't begin to imagine the pain. When we arrived, a grief like I've never experienced was unleashed.

The victim advocates—volunteers provided through the police department—were already there, and they helped us make a plan to go to my sister and to my dad and stepmom. The police had been unsuccessful in finding my dad because he was building a new condominium and temporarily living with my stepmother's mom, Grandma Jo. We tracked my dad down, and Craig, his voice shaking as much as his hands holding the phone, asked my dad to meet him at Grandma Jo's house.

Forever etched into my mind is Grandma Jo seeing us come up the steps and announcing our arrival with her warm smile. "It's Craig and Sher!" How quickly her face crumpled as she realized something was wrong. My stepmom emerged from the living room, her face changing from fearful to pure pain as she rushed into the kitchen where my dad was sitting at the table with his hands folded like he already knew. When we told them the news, his wail was a sound that I will never forget. This was not their first rodeo in the arena of losing children. She and Dad had lost her son only four years earlier to a car accident—along with losing her oldest daughter to an illness twelve years ago. This pain was not new to them. I absolutely hated telling them this devastating news.

Ever since my stepbrother had been killed, I'd been living life hanging on to this idea that even though my brother had a wild streak, he was protected. Nothing bad would happen to him because there was no way that God would take my brother after my dad and stepmom had already lost one son. God doesn't do that to parents. A rage built inside me, stemming from my instant need to blame someone for this horrible tragedy. I chose to blame God.

The next few days were full of funeral preparations, visits from a steady stream of supportive friends and family, and darkness. Incredible darkness. In the few moments I could steal away I would sit in my closet with my head on my knees and my hands held tightly over my mouth to silently wail, to plead with God that this all be a bad dream.

When I picture this scene in my mind, I always ask myself, Where was the booze? It was nowhere to be found. In fact, I don't recall drinking or even thinking about drinking at all during that time. I couldn't do that to my family. My kids needed their mom and my parents needed their daughter. Most important, my husband and I needed each other. Craig had lost one of his best friends in my brother. We were both grieving this huge loss.

My ability to avoid drinking during this time brings truth to the fact that the descent into addiction is slow and calculated. I hated alcohol then; it was part of my brother's story. He and his best friend had made the decision to party and then get into a car and drive it to their deaths.

ಬಿಬಿಬಿ

These memories all come rushing back to me as I hold my Mom through her tears. She's shattered, and all of a sudden, the hard days on the recent ride seem insignificant when I realize what my mom had been going through while I was gone. My heart aches for her as I think about the road ahead.

21

Uncovering the Dirt

It's the day before Thanksgiving, and I'm busy preparing for the feast tomorrow. I always cook my turkey the day before, which takes so much stress off the inevitable timing of food that accompanies a major holiday. My dear friend and Ride4Life buddy, Bonnie, is sitting at my counter as I peel a massive pile of potatoes. It's a peaceful day with my friend and my food in my kitchen, which is my favorite place since our remodel this past summer.

After saying goodbye to Bonnie, I linger on the front porch and just chill in the beautiful Indian summer day. It may sound like I'm in a totally happy place, and I kind of am, but I also have a decision to make. Do I run to the store and get vodka to stash away over the holiday?

A normie wouldn't see the real issue I'm mulling over. I won't be able to go to the store on Thanksgiving Day, and the thought of not having alcohol in the house just in case—it made me very uneasy. Sometimes just knowing a drink is available eases my anxiety.

The other issue is that I really don't want to drink today, but this rare occurrence isn't known to always be so strong by five p.m. If I have alcohol in the house I might open it, and I'm not sure if I can maintain the control I need for the holiday.

118

Thanksgiving Eve, aka "Blackout Wednesday," used to be a favorite night for imbibing in years past. Whoever came up with the brilliance that mashed potatoes are ideal to quell a hangover deserves credit. However, I don't want to drink to the blackout stage—I need to be at the top of my game for the sake of the family holiday tomorrow.

I take a break from my inner debate to answer the phone. I don't recognize the number, so I answer with a quizzical "Hello?"

"Is this Sherry?" the pleasant voice on the line asks.

My heart sinks, and I sit down hard on the porch steps. This can't be good.

The caller identifies herself as a nurse at the hospital my stepdad is in. My mom has been there around the clock, but the report this morning had been rather positive. "Sherry, your mom needs you to come to the hospital right away," the nurse states in a calm, quiet voice.

"Does she need a ride?" I ask. "I'm confused. Everything was fine this morning when I talked to her."

The nurse must detect the rising panic in my voice because when she speaks again, she says, "Your sister is on her way with her husband, and you should ride up with your husband as well."

I pull the phone away from my ear to see who's beeping in, and when I see it's Craig, I disconnect from the nurse. I ask Craig, "What is going on?!"

"It's Bob—not good. Be ready in ten minutes."

"OK," I say softly. Then, paralyzed in fear, I pray. But I don't know what to say. "Please, God. Please, God."

In a few moments I'm shaken out of this reverie and into practical mode. *Turkey! Do I take it out of the oven? Turn off the oven? Put it on low? What the heck—will we even have Thanksgiving?*

Within minutes Craig is here. "I don't know what to do about the stupid turkey!" I say through my tears.

"Let's just turn it way, way down," he calmly says. "Now, c'mon. We need to go."

When we get to the hospital, Bob is already gone save for the machines breathing for him. We hold my mom as she says goodbye to her best friend. Then we all gather at our house to begin the planning process for burying someone we loved.

About a week later I go to the cemetery by myself, sober. I'm battling an overwhelming desire to escape the darkness and get totally smashed—I have been ever since the funeral a few days ago. I don't like the scars; I can feel their roughness. These scars are better kept shut, but they don't stay shut unless you allow them to heal properly. I feel the edges of the scars that have been trying to reopen since Bob's funeral, and I have no desire to let that happen. I'm hoping that a visit to the cemetery will prevent this from happening. So, I go.

It's impossible not to stop first at my brother's grave. I pause in front of the headstone and gaze at his image etched on the stone. I impulsively smile back at his mullet hairstyle from the early nineties. The tree we planted has grown, and the winter grass is crunchy beneath me as I kneel to put my hand on the cold stone. There's no denying that it looks like a grave that's been there awhile. This saddens me as the awareness of how long he has been gone sets in. I fight a panic welling up inside. Every fiber in my body is being awakened to a horrific memory that I've tried for years to keep buried.

A memory as devastating as the death itself. It had occurred in this very spot.

October 1994

I wasn't ready to move back into the real world after Steve died.

Tangled memories of the days following his tragic death were full of family and friends passing through our doors. Meals appeared out of nowhere, and the clean dishes with Post-it notes identifying their owners took over an entire counter. Fairies in the form of friends flitted about, cleaning my house and running errands. They surrounded us with unbelievable love and care. Then the fairies were gone. The phone calls and casseroles dwindled in frequency, and somehow Craig went back to work and the kids went back to school. "A schedule will be good," the fairies said. "We have to go back to our lives and so must you."

The hardest part about sudden loss is that when it happens you're surrounded, but you're still in shock and then the shock starts to wear off. Everyone moves on with their lives, and you can't seem to put one foot in front of the other because each foot is so heavy.

The soil around our home is clay, and the way I felt reminds me of when my kids would get stuck in it. The clay would cake their little boots, and they'd give up and leave the boots behind only to become immobilized again as their stockinged feet got stuck, and then they'd worm their way out of their socks to be barefoot in the clay. This time when the mud sucked them in, they couldn't go any farther and would call for help. This is what I should have done when my soul was being sucked in down to the bare skin. Instead I chose to stay stuck with nothing left but tears. Tears that I hid as the darkness sucked me in.

It was late October when our kids asked if they could go to Wednesday night church. They were sick of the quarantine I'd declared on our lives. I didn't have a good reason to say no except that I had been avoiding all things church since the funeral. I just didn't want to socialize, evangelize, or moralize with anyone. I wasn't up for a "how are you doing," "good to see you," or "praying for you" kind of conversation.

"Maybe your dad can take you," I told Abby and Loren. That idea went south when Craig came in the door earlier than usual. One look at him told me why. He was ghostly pale with flushed cheeks and eyes barely open. A dreaded man-cold was upon us. Craig went straight for the couch as the kids, oblivious to his illness, clamored around him.

"Daddy, can you take us to church? Mom said it was OK!"

I rolled my eyes at no one but the wall as he told them he was very sick and maybe I would take them. So we made a deal, the kids and me. I would drop them at the side door and come back to the same side door to pick them up. "Mommy will *not* be coming in and will be at the same side door when your classes are done. Do we understand each other?"

They nodded at me in agreement, and after a quick dinner we were on our way out the door. As I was leaving, Craig called out, "Hey, hon, don't stop at the cemetery yet, OK?"

"I'm not planning on it," I replied, but after the kids were dropped off, I felt kind of peaceful. It was a beautiful night, and I wasn't in a hurry to head home to my couch-ridden husband. *Maybe I should go to the cemetery*, I thought, totally ignoring my husband's request. My mind made up, I drove the short distance and parked on the road, unsure if I was going to get out of the car.

C'mon, Sherry, do this. I got out and strode toward the grave. *If I face this, maybe I can do a better job of getting on with life.* My purposeful stride was abruptly halted as I stopped suddenly and squinted my eyes toward Steve's grave. It was easy to spot amid the perfectly groomed grass; his was a mound of dirt signifying a more recent burial, so I knew it was his. But I was confused.

Looking at the mound of dirt, I felt a flurry of relief, excitement, and pure joy flood through me. It had all been a bad dream and I was waking up from this horrible nightmare! I ran toward the grave and stood on the edge of the dirt, shaking my head in amazement. A foot and leg were sticking out on one side and an arm and hand on the other. *Steve's trying to get out? So this has all been a joke? A nightmare?*

All this felt like too much to process, but it was what I'd been hoping for. *This makes no sense.* I was euphoric about what I was seeing and didn't want to think it was anything but hopeful. *I must bring this evidence home for Craig to see.* I couldn't risk bringing him back and the evidence disappearing. Clawing at the dirt, I freed the body parts gathered them close to me, mud and all. I kept the proof on my lap as I sped home to share my discovery with Craig.

I burst through the door, clutching my treasures to my chest, and ran into the living room, leaving a trail of mud in my wake. "Craig, Craig! Wake up! Look at this. I know you told me not to go, but I did. *And what if I hadn't?* It was all a bad dream or a joke or something. I don't know, but it doesn't matter!"

The look on Craig's face was total horror laced with confusion, and I understood why. "I know, right? This is crazy, but crazy *good*! We have to call people!" And with that I dropped the muddy body parts and ran for the phone. I was debating who to call first and faltering a little with what to say when Craig came up behind me and gently took the phone away.

"What are you doing?" I said rather shrilly and tried to grab it back.

He stopped me. "I need you to explain where you went and what you think you found."

I quickly filled him in on my cemetery detour, but when it came to my discovery, I had a hard time explaining. "When I saw the foot, I felt like I was waking up from a bad dream. That none of this was true. It's not true, right?" I said hopefully as I felt the familiar dread once again make itself at home inside me.

"You don't believe me," I said sadly because I was starting to doubt my story as well. The shock was wearing off, and as reality crept in I knew that I wasn't making sense of it either.

Craig put his feverish lips to my brow. "It's a joke. A horrible, sick joke, but our Steve is still gone. You know that, right?" In that moment I hated him for destroying my last hope that this grief was something I could wake up from, but I knew he was right. An insensitive prank had temporarily taken over my perception of reality, but the verdict would not be overturned. Steve was still dead. I had no choice but to accept that I'd never wake up from this nightmare.

November 2012

As I stand at the cemetery reflecting, I remember how the rest of that painful evening played out: getting someone to find the kids who had planted the fake body parts as a Halloween prank, reporting the tampering of a fresh grave to the police, and finally showering to rid myself of the dirt caked under my fingernails and flaking on my elbows. Then I went to bed and cried myself to sleep.

Why didn't I drink that night? Did I even think about it? It would've made sense to drink any time after Steve's accident.

I don't know why I didn't. The alcoholic I am today can't fathom that I didn't want to drink. All I know is that I am not that same woman today. *Today I am a woman who drinks too much.*

With that thought, I leave the cemetery and go to the liquor store for the thing I count on to keep my scars from opening.

PART 8

CONVICTED

They tried to make me go to rehab, but I said no, no, no.
—Amy Winehouse

22

Happy Birthday, I'm Sorry

Journal Entry, December 26, 2012

Thus ends my first sober Christmas, the first I can recall in a very long time. I'm on day seven of sobriety, and I'm looking back at the insane timeline of my decisions that have led me to another day one.

I need to look back at this when temptation strikes. I need to be able to capture how I felt in each moment that led me to a drink. I want to recognize the warning signs that indicate I am about to throw away the day's responsibilities and drink instead. Right now, the first impulse I am feeling is to stop taking the Antabuse pill. Craig is already getting lax and has forgotten to give it to me on a few mornings. I could easily just lie and tell him I took it anyway. For today, I don't want to pretend. I'm finding comfort that something else is in control of me because I'm not very good at it. And I'm tired. So tired of lies and the drama surrounding the decision to drink.

I know in my heart that I can do all things sober if I have to. It's just getting my head to agree when I hit the wall of my will. In the midst of detoxifying myself from five fifths of vodka in four days, I've done many things by stoically placing one foot in front of the other on this very narrow balance beam of my life.

1. *Three days into sobriety I went to the bar. My son and his sweet girlfriend who went on the bike ride from hell this past year got engaged! The after-party was at a bar downtown where I raised a glass of Diet Coke and toasted the newly engaged couple.*

2. *Christmas Eve and Christmas Day, I put on an Oscar-worthy performance of a sober wife and mom. I was genuinely sober but not genuinely happy about it and felt pretty horrible physically as well.*

3. *I went to work and got caught up after being gone for a week. I was able to put my fears to rest that I was going to get called out on my sick leave and have to admit it was all self-induced.*

4. *I've exercised every day. This never happens during the holidays, much less while I'm actively drinking.*

ೞೞೞ

My new sober date is Craig's birthday, December 19, 2012. Poor guy comes home expecting everything ready to go for the party at my dad's. He wants to come home to the gifts wrapped and ready for transport in the hallway. To the smell of my appetizer contribution to the party cooling on the stove. He wants to sneak a taste and have me slap his hand away and say, "It's for the party!" None of the above happens.

Instead Craig finds me lying on the couch. "Not better yet?" he asks from the doorway to the living room. I notice a touch of sarcasm laced with a little edge in his voice.

"No," I say rather dramatically as I lay my head back down on the pillow. I feel the hard lump of an empty bottle under the couch cushion. I'm trapped without a supply for the night, unless my family all leaves me to go to the party.

"I'm staying home with you, then," Craig says.

There goes that idea. I protest a little, but he holds his ground and says, "I'm going to make us dinner and then we'll just have a quiet evening together."

"I'll probably just sleep."

"That's fine," he says with a half-smile. "I'll still be here for you."

I do not deserve him.

After the kids are out the door, he comes in and sits on the ottoman in front of me. He's in my personal space big time, and there's no escape from his searching eyes. "Want to tell me why you're really sick?" he asks sadly, locking my eyes with his.

"You know."

"I want you to say it," he says. "Say it."

So I do. I'm tired of fighting this alone and feel some relief when I say it. "Fine. I've been drinking for days and just can't stop."

"I know," he says. "I leave here every day wondering what I am going to come home to. My best day this week was when I was sick myself and could just sleep and not think about how you are destroying our lives, our marriage, this family!" He has tears in his eyes. "You know life really sucks when a sick day is your best day."

The tears start falling down my cheeks and I open my mouth to speak, but he holds his hand up to quiet me.

"But you're choosing this—every single day. It's insane, just insane."

I had no words, no defense. I just sit there and sob.

After sitting there watching me sob for a few minutes without speaking, he takes my hand. "It's a very sick person who chooses to do this to someone on their birthday." With that, he walks into the kitchen and leaves me alone.

God, please help me. I'm so sorry, so sorry. I pray over and over, trying to work up the nerve to go to Craig. Eventually I move into the kitchen and he holds me as I sob.

"I just don't know how to stop," I say through my tears.

"Maybe you need to go to a rehab?" he suggests softly.

Mayday, Mayday! He just dropped the rehab bomb, and my answer to that is no, no, and no again. I have many reasons for my "Hell no, I won't go" attitude. How can I explain being gone for thirty or (gulp) more days? My kids will know I've been living a lie these past few years, not to mention my parents. And heaven forbid my coworkers at the ministry find out! No, rehab isn't an option today or any other day. With the exception of being gagged and bound to get there, I won't go to rehab.

Instead I tell Craig that I'll take over my own recovery and have tools to use when the impulse strikes. I know the impulses well, and they show up as the voice of the devil himself. I'll make a list of mantras to read when I hear the devil's voice whispering sweet nothings of boxed wine and little glass bottles. *They love you. They're your friend. No one will know if you have a little bit.* Then, quoting Jesus, I will say to the voices, "Get thee behind me, Satan."

"We can try it," Craig says skeptically. "But I feel like you've tried before on your own, and look where we are once again." We agreed to take it day by day along with the Antabuse, and he seemed content with that for now. We spend the rest of the night sitting close to each other and watching a movie while eating pizza. *Happy Birthday, Craig. I'm so sorry.*

The next morning, I complete my list of mantras to read when I'm tempted. Some seem shallow, but shallow works for me just as well as the deep stuff sometimes. It depends on the mood.

1. Courtney Cox is my age. A hot bod is possible if I take care of it (once I get it), and not drinking will get me there faster.
2. Packing for trips. How I hate packing and having everything be a size too small because I intended on losing ten pounds. This makes me feel depressed when I pack. Then I drink while I pack, and then—surprise! I open my suitcase when we get to our destination and, alas, a miracle has not taken place and still nothing fits. I'm limited in apparel during our stay. Sober packing will be harder, but at least I'll have clothes to wear.
3. Our sex life is in need of much more than the nonexistent effort I'm giving it. It might be helpful if I'm not passing out.

4. No more three a.m. wake-up calls when my body awakens in a cold sweat and screams for a drink.
5. I can start running. I mean, I don't right now, but I could if I wanted to.
6. I can write a book about overcoming alcoholism someday—or maybe a racy novel about a boozy housewife.
7. Don't go boating.
8. Sobriety is hard but maintaining my drinking life is harder.

23

The Boat, the Box, and the Blackout

June 2013

"Let them see you shine," I whisper into Olivia's ear as we say our goodbyes before the sun rises on this midsummer morning. Olivia is leaving on a mission trip with her youth group, and Craig and I are headed for a little getaway up north. With our boat in tow, which is also serving as a bike trailer, I'm eager for the next few days ahead.

I absolutely love any chance to head up to northern Michigan. The water in the many inland lakes is crystal clear with sandy bottoms. When you are boating, the shores are surrounded by dunes and rolling hills of orchards and wineries. The views from the bike paths are stunning and worth the required climbs.

Speaking of wineries . . . after six months of sobriety for me, Craig has "agreed" that it's OK to have a little wine this weekend—albeit his idea of a glass of wine is entirely different from mine, but hey, I can work with it. The wine conversation had happened about a week ago, and I had kept it very low-key, like I could not care less if I drank or not (when in reality it had been on my mind quite a bit lately).

ෂ෬෬෬

"Hey, hon?" I had said, looking up from my book and keeping my tone casual. "We are for sure taking the boat up north next weekend, right?"

"That's the plan," he replied without looking up from his laptop.

"I thought we could take our bikes too," I added and then, with a rehearsed tone, I threw my idea out to him. "Do you think it would be OK if I had some wine while we were there? I haven't drank in so long and thought maybe I could consider having some wine that weekend."

When he remained silent, I quickly added, "It's been sounding good, but not in a bad way. It just sounds relaxing."

"I suppose it would be fine," he said almost distractedly. "It depends on if you think it would be OK or not. We don't want to go backwards, do we?"

I'm not sure if this is a question I'm supposed to answer, so I decide to just smile and nod. Inwardly, I'm beaming!

৩৩৩

That conversation took place three days ago and I haven't taken even a sip of alcohol, even though I sort of have permission. Inside I'm a little impressed with myself. The old me (the one who carried a water bottle full of vodka in my purse) would've said, "If I'm drinking in a few days, then why wait?" Nope, not this time! I'm disciplined and playing by the rules.

We take our time as we drive north, stopping whenever the spirit moves us. "If this is empty-nesting, Mr. Hoppen, I think we're going to be OK," I tell Craig with a wink. We eventually settle in at a quaint lodge on Lake Leelanau that has a spot to dock our boat. Hand in hand, we walk into town, do a little window shopping, and contemplate which restaurant to choose for dinner.

Outwardly I appear relaxed as we swing our hands like a young dating couple. Meanwhile, my mind is screaming, *I don't care about the food! Just pick something!* My mouth is watering as I ruminate on how close I am to a glass of wine. Virtually minutes—oh, the joy of it! After a six-month dry spell, it sounds absolutely delightful.

"What are you hungry for?" Craig says, pointing to a little restaurant we're approaching.

"Looks good. Italian is always good with me!"

We decide on pizza for dinner and, to my relief, the waitress reviews the list of drink specials. I mean, what if they don't have alcohol in this pizza joint? I politely decline anything from the list of drinks laden with hard liquor and sugar, asking instead, "Do you have a local red?" Spoken just like a normal drinker would. Craig follows up my request with a beer for himself, and there you have it. We're both drinking. Just a normal couple out for dinner in a lovely lakeside town because—again—I'm a normal drinker. That binging and hiding crap is behind me, and we're moving into new territory.

When the waitress sets the glass in front of me, I silently count to forty-seven (my current age) so as not to look too eager then curl my hand around the familiar stem of the wine glass. *Here it goes.* I take a sip and silently toast new, normal-drinking me. When I set down the empty glass a whole thirty minutes later, I immediately want another but play by my rules. I am now a normal drinker. One is enough (for now), and I don't want to set off any alarms on Craig's radar. We walk back to the lodge hand in hand under the contented spell of a couple who just had a nice dinner and *one* drink.

I'm peaceful and I know why. If anyone were to ask me, "Where is this new peace you are feeling coming from?" I'd lie and say something like, "Sobriety for the win!" or "My peace comes from the Lord and his rich blessings in this new life of recovery."

There isn't any truth in either of those statements. My peace isn't from the contented happiness of a pleasant night out together. This inner calm and contentedness lies in knowing

I don't have to keep wondering when I'll drink again. The constant drama of the alcohol conversation in my head is gone.

Am I an alcoholic or possibly just someone who has to be careful? Will I break the sober streak today? When I go to the bank will I find myself in the liquor store parking lot?

I did good, right? I'm not freaking out that I can't keep drinking. Given the opportunity, I'd bathe in Merlot right now! But I stuck with one glass; it didn't kill me. What self-control, Sherry!

I know in my heart that this discipline doesn't come from my own noble self and my newfound talent of self-control. I don't want Craig to start worrying that allowing wine back into our lives is a bad idea. I'm not going to screw this up.

The next morning, we ride bikes to town to get supplies for a day of boating. We're limited to how much we can get because we have to carry our load back on our bikes. With our truck hooked up to the boat and with limited choices for parking, biking is our best option.

We buy an assortment of dips and chips and then I casually say—in a well-rehearsed tone—"Let's get some wine." I proceed to walk over to the wine section and hoist a box of white zin off the shelf.

Craig looks at me skeptically. "A box? Let's just get a bottle."

I roll my eyes. "Like a breakable bottle? Glass? On a bike? Not a good idea, Craig." Then I add, "Besides, then we have to come up with a corkscrew," hoping none of this sounds too rehearsed. I've been preparing for this little one-act play for a few days.

He still looks unconvinced, so I threw out my best line that I've been saving just in case I encountered any resistance. "Besides, it's way cheaper than an expensive bottle, which is all they have here in wine valley." I couldn't care less about where the grapes were grown. I care about running out of wine while on the boat.

"I guess," Craig says reluctantly, and before he changes his mind I head for the checkout.

While he unlocks our bikes, I pull an empty backpack out of my bike bag with the flourish of a magician. "Voilà!" I exclaim.

"You thought of everything, didn't you?" says Craig, looking more puzzled than impressed.

After carefully storing the chips, crackers, dips, cheeses, and paper goods in my bike pannier, I attempt to wrestle the box of wine into my backpack. I'm starting to sweat from the effort; it simply won't fit. However, I'm resourceful and determined. I carefully assess the situation and conclude the box is the problem, and who needs the box anyway? I walk over to the trash bin and tear the box away from the bulging bag of wine inside. "And there we go!" I say as I pack the foil bag with its spigot into my backpack.

"That works," says Craig with a slightly raised eyebrow.

We ride our bikes the short distance to the lodge, suit up and load the cooler with our purchases, and we're off for the day.

This summer day is Michigan at its finest. Warm, without a cloud in sight. A slight breeze keeps us comfortable, and my heart is full of joyous freedom in the moment. I'm itching to twist the spigot on the bladder of wine and get this party started, but I'm no fool. Even though I've been salivating over the thought of drinking since my one glass of wine at dinner last night, I know not to rush it. Oh, the sweet bliss of a boozy day upon me!

I make my move and casually busy myself opening dips and crackers, making a little spread on the cooler. To complete my performance, I set out two water bottles and two plastic cups from the hotel. I tear the tab off the spigot and am ready to pour.

"Already?" asks Craig.

I freeze. "Well, yeah, it sounds good with this." I gesture toward the picnic and continue pouring the wine. The plastics cups are so small that I feel like we're taking communion. "Cheers!" I say and tap his plastic cup with mine. The party is underway, and this is the last lucid memory I have of the day.

The Boat, the Box, and the Blackout

Every time Craig jumps in the water (which is often because it's hot), I grab and gulp, which leads to getting drunk very quickly. I recall a few things: great sex, a nap (aka passing out).

The light is dim when I wake up in the room at the lodge with two immediate thoughts: *Am I in trouble?* and *How the heck did we even get back here?* I glance out the window and can see our truck with the boat hitched to it. *Oh my God, we even trailered the boat. That is a two-man job! I am the other man. How did I do that?*

I remember nothing. My mind is a blank screen except for a few little blips here and there. Craig is still snoring away, so I do a little sleuthing and look around for the wine. *Dang, where is it?* I give up and sneak back into bed with him. When we wake up again, this time together, it is dark in the room and we're starving. The forlorn appetizers floating in the cooler look less than appealing, and there is one bottle of water floating chummily alongside the now-watery dips.

"Where's the wine?" I ask casually, pretending to organize the remainders of our picnic.

"You threw it in the trash," Craig says, looking at me carefully.

"Oh, that's right," I say, knowing immediately that I threw it away so he wouldn't feel the weight—or rather lack of it—and know that I'd been pounding the wine down like a drunken sailor all day.

I'm in shock that this happened again. Blackouts are the worst. I'd just had a solid six-month sobriety run around the track. I'd held the baton all by myself, and just like that I'd dropped it and had no one to blame but myself. Instead of admitting that my little experiment is a total bust, picking up my baton again, and asking my teammates for help to get back on track, I think about when I'll next be able to drink. And I'm furious at myself. I've been sober since December 19, 2012, and in one afternoon I've wrecked it! I did so many hard things, and here I am right back where I started.

"I'm going to shower," I say and duck into the bathroom to hide my tears of anger and frustration. I have two choices: one involves detoxing, hard work, and the will to stay sober, which I'm not feeling right now.

"I can't. I just can't," I whisper, burying my face in my hands. I know I'll go with plan B. I don't even consider the route of sobriety. In less than twenty-four hours I'm back to the stinking-thinking route that keeps me prisoner until I dig deep enough to release myself from daily binge drinking. I've fallen hard, and I'm deciding to just stay down on the ground for a while.

24

The Committee and the Compound

July 2013

Summer is flying by, I'm drinking *very* secretly, and so far I've not been found out. I may be drinking, but I'm also working hard on myself and my relationship with God—or rather he might be working on me. My *Jesus Calling* reading spoke to me this morning: "Take a walk on the high road with me."

I'm taking the higher road more often than not these days. I cannot afford to screw up and drink too much because my son is getting married! This wedding is too important to my son and so many others, and by the way? The ceremony is happening in our front yard!

"Hoppen, party of three hundred?" I like to call that out to remind everyone that this is a really big deal and all hands are needed on deck. But I also feel valuable and appreciated. Being busy works for me, especially when I'm in charge. Love it! My future daughter-in-law, Stephanie, is relying on me to pull off this front-yard bash, and my son is kind of aloof, just saying, "Mom's got it all under control."

For today she does.

೮೪೮೪೮೪

139

Sober Cycle

When I'm tempted to drink I have a little process, kind of a ritual, that is helping me to ride the crave wave. I talk to the committee.

The committee is all of these voices in my head who like to chime in with an opinion when I'm struggling with the drama of "to drink or not to drink." They all have a different dialogue, so I've labeled them appropriately. The committee is composed of the following groups:

PARTIERS:
Whoa, you deserve a drink. Look at what you're doing this summer—so much! Training for the Ride4Life and planning the wedding? You deserve a vodka on the rocks for good behavior!

NAYSAYERS:
You might as well drink because you probably will at some point. You kind of suck at long-term commitment. You'll probably fail anyway. Just give in and pour yourself a drink.

INTELLECTUALS:
Let's look at the numbers. In 2012, you were sober for 123 out of 365 days. Now here we are in 2013, and you've had 174 sober days before last month's boat day gone bad. You were halfway through the year already! That's a 51-day increase over last year's total sober days. You're so far ahead of the drinking game for 2013, so don't be hard on yourself. In 2014 you can make it your goal to increase that number of sober days even more.
(Obviously the intellectuals are good at math.)

THERAPISTS:
Sherry, what are you feeling right now? There must be a good reason you're dealing with this inner struggle. Why don't we talk?

TWELVE-STEPPERS:
Don't forget to let go and let God! One day at a time! If nothing changes, nothing changes. It works if you work it!
(This group knows every AA slogan ever said.)

NUNS:
Don't drink a drop, ever.
(The nuns are a quiet bunch.)

As the wedding day approaches, I'm not drinking at all and not even contemplating it much. The committee must be on summer break because I don't hear from them often. We're crazy busy and having fun at the same time. I am calling it "stressful fun" getting everything just perfect for the bride and groom. At the end of each day I'm exhausted and just want to go to bed.

On the day of the wedding the sun comes out around noon and melts away the gray and misty fog that had refused to burn off for the last three days. The sun bursts out, and the stage that is our front yard looks stunning and ready for action. I'm so grateful that we have such a wonderful day and it all happened without a glitch!

We dance, we laugh, we cry, and we celebrate the newlyweds until the wee hours of the morning. The darkness provides a curtain of protection from us seeing the actual mess we have to clean up the next day. In this moment our front yard is lit up by the stars, and the moon is reflecting off the pond. Magical! The wooden dance floor is empty, but the tent above is still twinkling from the thousands of lights strung throughout. There on that dance floor, at about three a.m., Craig asks me to dance. We cherish this moment together that belongs only to us: the parents who just let go of a child (and survived). It's such a joyous moment filled with so much raw emotion. I'm grateful to feel every bit of its beauty and grateful to be sober in it.

After the wedding, though, my story takes a familiar twist. I spend the next week drinking when I feel like it, timing my drinks with when I think I can get away with it. After a week of feeling like crap and sick of hangovers, I decide to take a break from the bottle. I'm also tired of feeling like I'm not accomplishing anything. We're heading into another big weekend as Labor Day approaches. It's time to empty out our little park model on the lake for the last time. We've sold it, and I couldn't be more ecstatic. I'll miss my neighbors, but that's the extent of any loss I'm feeling because I'm excited to move on. We've been looking at a certain cottage on Lake Michigan these past few months. It needs a ton of work, but that isn't the reason this potential cottage has me freaking out. It's in a Christian compound. Literally.

OK, it's not really a compound. It's a Christian organization that is family-oriented, with kids' activities and sessions with speakers for the adults. Incidentally, its name is Maranatha—this is where the Ride4Life had started and ended last year. It would be the same this year. They have a lodge where families stay for a week at a time—kind of a Christian camp for the entire family. The women residents (cottage owners like we would be) have an organized group all their own. They have prayer coffees and do good deeds all summer long.

I know I cannot be a part of any of this. I simply don't belong. If the other women knew my secret (and the thought of it being a secret at that camp sounds exhausting), they would not let me into their club. If the sale of this cottage goes through, it will come with a price. What kind of price do you put on playing pretend?

I hadn't paid much attention to this gated community until my potential cottage was just beyond those gates. I wasn't obsessing about this purchase like I usually am when I really want something. I am known to be ruthless when it comes to being pushy about what I want. Not that Craig gave in easily. But we're on the same page for once and wading through the pros and cons of lakefront living while putting it in God's hands over and over.

After Labor Day I go into full Ride4Life prep mode both at home and at work. I'd forgotten, perhaps intentionally, that I have a mammogram scheduled for September ninth, the day before my forty-seventh birthday. Who does that? I have so much going on that I don't want to take the time to go. I consider canceling until a voice from the committee chimes in (apparently there is now a medical team on the committee). It appears the committee members have opinions on more than just drinking, and they encourage me not to cancel.

I know why I'm not canceling the appointment, but it's a reason I refuse to let surface for the public eye (read: Craig). It isn't the fear of the actual mammogram; it's the fear of the mammogram results.

Two years prior I had gone through the suspicious-result process and a biopsy. Not the most pleasant experience, but when I heard that everything was fine, it was such a relief after ten days of hellish worry about results that kept leading to another test and then another. Of course I'd googled everything I could think of relating to breast cancer and was horrified to find out that the stats on drinking's relationship to breast cancer were not good. The odds were not in my favor, to say the least.

"How was your day?" Craig asks as we sit down for dinner on September ninth.

"Kind of yuck." I shrug. "Mammo day isn't really all that great."

"Everything OK?"

"Well, I didn't get a phone call right away, so that's a good sign, I think. Can we just not talk about it? I'll worry about it when there is something to worry about."

This isn't exactly true. Last time I'd promised God that if he would spare me from breast cancer, I'd quit drinking. *Please God, no! Not my boobs and my hair! They're my best features.* God spared me, and I not only kept my boobs and hair but I also kept my drinking problem. Now I'm a little uneasy knowing that I haven't kept my promise.

The day before the Ride4Life 2013 departure, which would be my fourth ride, I get a letter in the mail. "My boobs are fine!" I say, waving the letter of good results at Craig when he comes in the door.

"Good deal!" he says, kissing me on the forehead. "And good timing too. Now you can keep your mind on the road."

I'm grateful not to be dealing with this as I ride seven hundred miles around Michigan. Again. That night I lie in bed thinking. *How can this be my fourth Ride4Life, and how can drinking still be a problem?* I've come a long way from that hungover, inexperienced, and scared cyclist heaving in the gas station restroom, but something still holds me back. The drinking. A fear has been building that I'm missing out on whatever God has planned for my life, that every time I drink, I'm taking a step back from that plan. I know I'm stuck until I move forward into a permanently sober life.

God is working in me; I know this without a doubt. I feel him pulling me in to his arms and then, like a constrained child, I struggle to free myself. I have so much to sober up for, but no person, place, or thing can save me from this addiction. Only God. It's all God.

These days I feel like I'm grieving a huge piece of myself that's been lost for a long time—or possibly was never free. I need freedom from alcohol to find my way back to myself. To be who I really am. So why can't I make the choice to say I'm done with drinking? There isn't any place in my life that alcohol belongs.

Tears drip onto my pillow. I know I've drawn closer to God, even while drinking has still been a part of who I am. He's loving me through it, but I want more than love—I want him to save me. *Take this cup, Lord. Take this cup.*

I think about receiving the test results and reading that there wasn't any cancer to worry about. I was surprised. Again. *Why do you keep giving me a break, Lord? Why do you keep saving me? What are you saving me for?*

Like a mental movie reel, I remember all the times I woke up safe when I shouldn't have. I'm horrified by how many times I've drank so much that I shouldn't have ever woken up. The times that I drove drunk and woke up in my bed and have no idea how I got there. I think about every blackout I came back from. God is the God of second chances, and in my case many more chances after that.

All things are possible in me, I hear Him saying to my heart. His voice is getting louder, and I'm reminded again and again of the verse I wrote down earlier in the week: "You will seek me and find me when you seek me with all your heart" (Jeremiah 29:13 NIV).

I'm trying Lord, I'm trying.

෮෮෮

The Ride4Life 2013 is glorious. On the second day we hit a downpour, and I fight escalating anxiety as I flash back to last year's ride. We had a solid week of this nasty weather last year, and I physically fight to keep panic from welling up in me at the fear of that happening again. But my anxious moment passes just like the rain clouds. For the rest of the trip, we are blessed by mostly clear skies and minimal winds. I come home to the usual anticlimactic ending—except for a sweet surprise from my husband.

The kids are all there to see me ride in, and as they get ready to leave, Craig asks if they would like to go for a walk. This brings raised eyebrows because we're not a family who strolls along together. Maybe a run or a bike ride where it can be called a race and someone can win, but not just a walk. Therein also lies the reason we don't play games together. We're a competitive bunch.

Everyone agrees, willing to humor Craig. I have a sneaking suspicion that this was going to end well, but I play along as if I don't suspect anything. We walk about a quarter mile down the road leading to Lake Michigan and through the gate, stopping at a driveway.

"OK guys, look up!" Craig is wearing a huge smile. "We're going to make lots of memories here." Then he whispers in my ear. "They said we can go in and show the kids. I signed the offer yesterday."

This year's Ride4Life has dissipated all my concerns about living in this community. I'm so excited to show our kids that I don't even feel my screaming calves protest as we climb the forty-seven stairs to the front door. We're greeted by an awful smell and pull our shirts over our noses to muffle the rank smell of the previous owner's dogs, which had been inside too long and not cleaned up after.

"We're gutting it completely," Craig assures them. I can see the potential. Smells and outdated decor aside, it's an amazing space with huge windows showcasing stunning lake views.

"I can't believe it," I tell Craig.

"New beginnings." He kisses me.

Even now, though, in my mind is always the drinking. *I wonder if I can ever be sober here? Will I be good enough for this community of Christians?* I do a quick tally. *We're set to close by the end of this month, and then with thirty more days before we get the keys, that brings me to about November first.*

I must think this through. I don't want to drink here. Unlike our former place at Sandy Pines, this one won't be closed in the winter. It would be a winter getaway for us as well. I felt my heart pound a little faster knowing that if I were to achieve said sober goal, it couldn't be just a summer fling.

Two days later I find myself in the Monday morning calm of home after everyone else has left for work and school. I need to spend time talking with God; I have questions for him.

How do I know that I'm done drinking? I haven't in a while and am wrestling with a temptation to drink one more time as a goodbye to it. Focusing on Proverbs 3 this morning in my devotions, it shook me up—and that's an understatement. Verse 5 is written for me:

> Trust GOD from the bottom of your heart;
> don't try to figure out everything on your own.
> Listen for GOD's voice in everything you do, everywhere you go;
> he's the one who will keep you on track.

I'm guilty of not trusting him with the possibility of a life without alcohol. Every single time I take matters into my own hands, I fall short. For me, that is taking a drink.

Paging through journal after journal of the past few years, my heart aches. It's all there in black and white—so obvious. I've been running from God for a long time. This sobering thought sinks into every fiber of my being and starts the tears again. I sit alone in the dim light of early morning and feel so moved by God's presence that I'm scared. Not of God himself, but scared that I know what he's asking me to do and I'm not ready.

"Get in my presence," he lovingly whispers.

੪੪੪

What happens when we live God's way? He brings gifts into our lives, much the same way that fruit appears in an orchard—things like affection for others, exuberance about life, serenity. We develop a willingness to stick with things, a sense of compassion in the heart, and a conviction that a basic holiness permeates things and people. We find ourselves involved in loyal commitments, not needing to force our way in life, able to marshal and direct our energies wisely. (Galatians 5:22–23)

It's clear as I spend time reading through all I've written these past few years that I'm guilty. Guilty of making my own rules and turning away from what God is trying to do in me. I'm like Jonah, running from God. *At least I didn't end up in the belly of a whale—just on a bike.*

PART 9

LOVED

25

The Perfect Crime

The perfect crime has five elements:

- A Plan—How are you going to carry it out?
- Timing—Carefully choose a time when you won't be caught in the act
- Tools—Gather everything you need
- Cleanup—Allow ample time to get rid of any evidence
- Consequences—Be prepared that there will be some even if you aren't caught

I am planning the perfect crime for the upcoming weekend. I am intoxicated just thinking about it. Hoppen, party for one? Why yes, that's me!

My plan is falling into place so perfectly I'm almost giddy about it. I have to remind myself not to sound too enthused around Craig. His radar has been on high alert lately, and I know he's been suspicious of the possibility of my drinking at times. Rightfully so, I guess, but he can't prove anything. I think he wants to take off so badly this weekend that he has looked the other way a few times.

It's *that* time of year here in Michigan. Hunting season. That means guys stay at the cabin all weekend, and I will be alone for the entire weekend. As timing would have it, my youngest is going away on a college visit, and that leaves me gloriously alone with a bottle (or two) of Red Popov. Glorious, just glorious.

Is Red a new friend you might ask? Why no, Red is not new at all! Red is the last of my liquid friends to hang around. Red is clear, practically odorless, and a far cry from White Zin, who replaced its predecessor Captain Morgan years ago. I quit sailing with the Captain when eyebrows started to arch in suspicion concerning my drinking, and the smell of the Captain is hard to hide.

I have a pattern of replacing my drink of choice as quickly as I do my friends when they start to cause problems. I choose only those who don't question my decisions, meaning they don't call me out on my drinking. Those who do are not invited to my parties with Red anymore, thus explaining my now much smaller circle of friends. These so-called friends had started to question my relationship with some of my liquid friends, and somebody ultimately had to go.

Why can't we all just get along? It's like being in middle school where you could have only one best friend, and heaven forbid someone else try to hang out with the two of you. It just doesn't work. Someone always gets mad, there's a fight— usually followed by tears—and you have to ask someone to leave the group. One by one my friends have slipped away due to the confrontations and arguments as they felt the threatening presence of Red.

"Red has to go," they would say to me, appearing concerned.

Red would say, "Hell to the no!" and I would nod my head in agreement. Red is easy to be with, requiring little to no conversation, and doesn't mind if I fall asleep while binge-watching endless episodes of *The Office*. If I am feeling down and feel a good cry coming on, Red is there to console me. Red builds me up and makes me feel secure, self-confident, and even a little bit sassy. I hate it when I really want to hang out with Red but have to say, "I can't. You aren't invited, Red."

Not everyone welcomes Red. So when I'm alone, I always call and invite only Red over.

Late Friday afternoon I say my goodbyes to Craig, and he just has to add, "Promise me you will behave." He says this with one hand on the doorknob, ready to bolt. I can see he's working just as hard to hide his excitement about hunting as I am about my party plan. His head is already sitting around the fire drinking beer and eating beef jerky (the wife of any hunter has the power to see these things).

"Of course," I say, rolling my eyes. It's not a lie! I didn't say that I wouldn't drink, just that I would behave. Both are possible. Olivia's ride shows up next, and after a hug goodbye I am deliciously alone.

I assemble a tray with chips, dip, and peanut M&M's. After all, it is happy hour. My first shot of the night settles into me like a warm blanket of comfort. Not bothering with a mixer of any kind, I throw back another and settle in with the remote. The party is underway, and in this moment I am content. The bliss of finally being able to freely drink brings me back into the kitchen to frequent the shots a little more often than usual. I tell myself it is because I'm enjoying myself, but I'm also a wee bit aware of trying to alleviate guilt over my deceit. I tell my guilty conscience that I'm not hurting anyone, trying to tranquilize it so it won't creep in and temper my fun. The party only lasts until about ten p.m. and then BAM! I am out cold.

I wake up around three a.m. and find myself awkwardly sprawled in the recliner. *Why does this always happen?* I hate remedying this unwelcome three-a.m. alarm. Past experience has shown me that the only way to stop my pounding heart, anxious for what I don't understand, is to drink.

Just a nip to get back to sleep. I hate this. I don't know of a way to avoid drinking in the middle of the night. That shot is always accompanied by the same daunting thought. *Anyone who drinks in the middle of the night is for certain a raging alcoholic.* I drink just to get rid of that thought alone!

Sober Cycle

When I reach for the bottle it feels lighter than I think it should, and I'm a little concerned at how much of the fifth is already gone. *I have to control my intake a little. I mean, I promised to behave.* In this moment though, I feel I have no option other than to tip back the rest of it and go to bed.

The sun pours into my bedroom window and directly on my face. Very brightly. *Coffee. I need coffee.* I slowly make my way down the stairs. While I wait for the coffee to brew, I rummage around for the extra bottle of Red I'd purchased. No way this girl is risking a drive to the liquor store. I know that is always a horrible idea but somehow, when under the influence, it seems not so bad. I've learned to prevent the possible DUI by being well-stocked.

I'm busting into a new bottle kind of early. I hope I have enough for the rest of the weekend. I better slow it down a little. I fill a juice glass and decided to top it off with a little OJ just to make drinking this early seem a little more civilized.

Mimosa anyone? Never mind, there isn't any champagne. I drink it straight and fast and settle into the recliner with my coffee and journal. I doze off briefly without writing a word and wake up feeling anxious and unsettled. I fill my juice glass again and toss it back, hoping to quickly alleviate the uneasiness. I can't put my finger on what doesn't feel right.

It's like I'm drinking without any of the benefits. Besides feeling anxious, my stomach feels queasy. *Maybe I'm coming down with something.* Up to bed I go to sleep away whatever "this" is. I go to sleep (or pass out) almost immediately only to wake up again less than an hour later.

What the heck? I feel shaky and a little dizzy and want to go back to sleep in the worst way just to escape this dreadful feeling. I am not moving, but it feels like the bed is. I feel my heart start to pound. A feeling of unease starts in the pit of my stomach and creeps its way to my head. I break out in a panicked sweat. I feel a sense of foreboding. *What is going on? Am I dying? Is this alcohol poisoning? Oh God, I don't want to die!*

154

These questions are racing through my head faster than I can answer them. *What do I do? I need to call someone! Who? Do I call 911? Hell, no!*

I try to calm down and feel myself start to hyperventilate. *What the hell is going on?* In a moment of my gripping fear teaming up with desperation, I text a friend who has bailed me out of my own problems a few times. I keep it vague just to see what happens. I tell myself if she responds, I will ask for help.

Hey there what you up to?

I really wanted to say, "Hey there, I think I am dying. Can you come over?"

I wait about ten minutes, not taking my eyes off the screen. *Please answer please please please.* But my phone refuses to ping with an answer from her. *She must be busy; she always answers.*

I try to calm myself by taking deep breaths and then decide to try another shot of vodka. This time my attempt to swig leads to the vodka immediately spewing out of my mouth in a spray of alcohol followed by a dash to the toilet and retching disgusting bile.

I go back to the kitchen, but I am at a loss what to do, and I sit down hard on the kitchen floor, put my head on my knees and start to sob. *What is going on?* I'm so scared, and the only way I know how to deal with fear—or any other emotion—is to drink. And it's not working.

I have to try again. I crawl over to the fridge and look for the magic mixer that might work to get the alcohol down. The only options are milk, flavored creamer, and prune juice. Desperate times call for desperate measures, and I pour a glass of half prune juice and half vodka and somehow gag it down. *Well, at least I will be regular!* I resume sitting on the floor with my back against the fridge and my head on my knees and just pray this horrid feeling will pass. *Dear God, help me.* It's all I can think to say.

I quickly google "How do I know if I have alcohol poisoning?" and read a forum of others asking the same question. Now I am terrified.

True or False: Anyone who passes out from drinking should "sleep it off."

FALSE. People can continue to absorb alcohol even after passing out, and this can lead to a fatal overdose of alcohol. Some unfortunate people left to sleep after becoming drunk "aspirate" their own vomit and choke to death. So, it's important to stay with someone who might have had too much to drink and not to assume that he/she will be fine after "sleeping it off." (Excerpt from "14 'Facts' About Drinking: Are You Misinformed?" CBS News, https://www.cbsnews.com/pictures/14-facts -about-drinking-are-you-misinformed/13/.)

I am going to die.

26

Good Friends Don't Let You ~~Drink~~ Get Sober Alone

A true friend never gets in your way unless you happen
to be going down.
—Arnold H. Glasow

The thought of dying from this or anything else terrifies me,
and I ask God again: *Lord, show me what to do.*

My heart is pounding somewhere down in the pit of my
stomach. I have to make a move, a decision of some sort, and
it should not be toward the bottle of vodka that is staring at me
from atop the counter.

I want to call Robin. *Now that would be a desperate move.* Also,
a bold move on my part because she has no reason whatsoever
to answer my cry for help. I definitely wouldn't if I were her!
I have been absolutely horrible to her since the moment she
became one who turned our friendship into a call to duty to
point out my faults concerning all things drinking.

Robin is the friend I have more history with than anyone
else outside of my family. On her fortieth birthday I gave her
a framed black-and-white photo of the two of us. We were
in first grade and sitting on the front steps of the elementary
school. Two little girls in all their polyester finery, innocent to
what the world had in store for their friendship. We were like

157

sisters as we grew up, sometimes hating the sight of each other but more often the best of friends.

We tried out for cheerleading together, and she did everything she could to help me make it. She made the team seven times and I, sadly, did not make it seven times. I was persistent but not coordinated, and no amount of coaching from Robin could change that.

I had two aspirations in high school. One was to be a cheerleader, which was an ultimate fail. The other was to be a writer. That would be a more easily achieved aspiration. My senior year I was the editor of our school newspaper, *The Excalibur*. A perk of this coveted position was being able to choose a coeditor, and of course I chose Robin. *The Excalibur* gave us an excuse to legitimately leave school almost every day.

We would concoct a list of potential errands that sounded legitimate enough to sign ourselves out in the office for "newspaper" stuff, leaving us free to go to McDonalds or wherever the mood took us that day. Our constant misuse of *The Excalibur* time always left us in a bit of a conundrum when it came time to publish the monthly edition. It wasn't like anyone was waiting with bated breath for it, but the newspaper was expected once a month. We would scramble for content and somehow pull it off, though there were a few times where my name was behind every article in the edition.

Robin taught me how to inhale my cigarette instead of faking it. She introduced me to name-brand clothes I couldn't afford and boys I shouldn't have hung out with. Later in life we sat at each other's kitchen tables, smoking and drinking coffee while our kids played together and trashed the house. Our friendship persevered as I wiped her tears after the heartbreak of miscarriage, and she was my rock when life took my little brother too soon.

This drinking thing though—it has destroyed our friendship. It doesn't matter if you are my lifelong friend or my husband of twenty-nine years. Don't try to get between me and my friend Red Popov.

Robin had given it a good effort, and she had lost. I was so focused on the fact that she could still drink and yet I was not supposed to that it made me blind to the place of love and concern she was coming from. So I cut her out of my life and did my best to ignore the ache of loss that comes with the end of forty-plus years of friendship. I had tried to fill the void, but what I had been using wasn't working anymore. I turned away from the glaring eye of the bottle on the counter and picked up my phone again.

This time, I call her instead of texting. Caller ID gave her a five-second warning that it was me calling out of the blue. She answers with a rather guarded hello. When I hear her voice, no words come. I start to sob, unable to talk, and when I finally do speak all I say is, "I need you. Please come."

Without any hesitation she replies, "I'll be right there." I stare at the phone in my hand, knowing I've made the call that will change everything. Booze has gotten me into some real trouble here. This day will not be taken lightly.

I make my way slowly to the front door and unlock it, leaving it slightly ajar so Robin will know to come right in. I crawl into bed, unaware of the way I smell or look, not caring in the least. It doesn't matter. This is the end, the rock bottom that everybody talks about. I might as well look (and smell) the part. I'm still scared, but I feel relief knowing that help is on the way.

A few minutes later I hear Robin open the door and yell, "Sher?" Her voice is full of concern. I don't answer. I can't— I'm crying so hard. She races up the stairs and then she is there, holding me. I'm sobbing uncontrollably with no sign of stopping.

"Scoot over," she says and climbs in the bed with me. This friend I don't deserve embraces me, stench and all, and we weep together. When the words do come from me, they spew out in a sobbing rant.

"I'm sorry, I'm so sorry I've been such a jerk. I've been lying to you, to everyone! I never quit—I just tried to hide it better. I've been so mad at you but mad at me more because I kept making this everyone else's fault. It's mine, all mine. I'm so sorry, I'm so sorry I wrecked us."

I can't quit saying I'm sorry. Robin just keeps hugging me and saying, "It's OK, it's OK you called me. I'm here. I'm not going to let you go." Her words and embrace make me feel safe, and I fall asleep.

Just before I fall asleep, I ask her to call another friend of ours. I need an army today, an army of angels, and God sent me two of them. I am kind of in and out of it for a while, but when I wake up they are both there, full of hugs and "Love you, Sher."

I'm not entitled to any of this, but I will be forever grateful that they are here. We have bursts of laughter, too, because I always have to make a joke out of something and there are a few laughable things happening.

The worst is my choice of apparel for hitting rock bottom. I have on ancient gym shorts and a ribbed men's tank undershirt. White, without a bra. Nobody wants to see that. We keep busting out at this extremely out-of-character look I have going. Not to mention I smell pretty rank. I'm glad they can laugh at that.

I might as well be Catholic as many secrets as I confessed that day, using my friends like a priest for confession. Then the gravity of my situation on this sunny Saturday would hit me again and the tears would start to flow. They hold me between them like the white of an Oreo and just let me cry. Actually, we spoon. What can I say—I'm incredibly needy today.

Later I wake up and it is just the two of us again. Robin is holding out a tray of meager offerings, basically whatever the heck she could find in my cupboards—which isn't much. As I try to choke down a few bites, she asks me, "Sher, where is the booze hidden?"

Without any hesitation I reply, "Top cupboard, next to the fridge, where all good Dutch people hide their liquor."

"Haha," she says. "Be right back." She goes downstairs and dumps it out.

Well, she did that rather unceremoniously. Seems like there should have been a drumroll or something. The late afternoon dusk is upon us. Robin has stayed with me all day.

"Sher, you need to think about getting it together before Olivia comes home."

I nod; I know she's right.

"Get in the shower—you'll feel better and smell better," she says with an exaggerated wrinkle of her nose.

"I feel a lot better. You can leave—I'll be OK." I know I'll be shaky, but I can tell I'm no longer in any danger of death by alcohol. She gets up from the bed to leave but pauses at the door.

"You need to promise me something."

"Whatever you want," I say. "I owe you that."

"Promise me that you will tell Craig what happened here today." Robin goes on to say that she and her husband will come help me talk to him if I need it. "It's time to move forward, Sher. You can do this."

I hug her at the door. "Thank you, thank you. I promise I will. It's time. You are right; I'm scared to death, Rob. I'm so scared, but I am going to do it this time."

And as I start to cry again, she gives me a last hug. "You got this."

I get in the shower quickly and put on my sweats (clean sweats). I'm making a good effort to look a little presentable for Olivia. The goal is to appear like I'm casually waiting for her while reading a book with a Diet Coke and some chips. But I have neither in my possession and thus starts another familiar train of thought. *Maybe I should go get some?*

That thought opens the door for some familiar thoughts to creep in. *If I run to the store, should I grab a pint? What if I need it and I don't have any?* This whole detox thing is freaking me out. *I have to go slow.* After all my googling I had read repeatedly that severe alcoholics should detox in a hospital. *That's not happening, so I should probably ease into it instead of totally cutting myself off.* Not that I hadn't done it on my own quite a few times these past few years. Still, being totally without during the night could bring all that heart-pounding anxiety back and I can't do that—I just can't.

Olivia is only thirty minutes away, so I make a quick decision and grab my purse and drive to the closest liquor store. I always avoid this store just in case I run into somebody I know. But that doesn't matter right now as desperation trumps convenience any day. *Dang, I've been desperate a lot today.* I have a small drink before Olivia gets home. *For medical reasons.*

Olivia walks in the door and I'm appropriately settled in my chair—a cup of coffee in my hand since, in my haste, I'd totally forgotten to grab a Diet Coke from the store—trying to look normal with a book open on my lap.

"Hey there," I say. "Tell me all about it!" My guilt makes me feel like she can see right through me.

"It was OK." She tells me a little bit about the college she visited and what she liked and didn't like in very vague terms. Obviously not interested in conversation, she stands up and says, "I'm tired and need a shower. I'm heading up," and leaves me alone once again.

"OK, I'm not far behind you." I'm dreading going to bed, knowing the three a.m. wake-up call is most likely scheduled.

⁊ɔ⁊ɔ⁊ɔ

I squint at my phone: 3:02 a.m. Right on schedule. *I don't even feel like I slept yet.* I must have, but I'm sleeping so fitfully anyway that I decided to forgo the liquid courage and just fight through it. I wake up the next morning grateful the night is over, and I wonder: *Will this be my first sober day? My last day one ever?* Standing there, waiting for the coffee to brew, I notice I have a voicemail from yesterday.

It's our Realtor telling me that our new cottage is completely available. The previous owners have everything out and the door is open for me to get the key off the counter. I better get on that—I can't just leave it standing open!

It's a beautiful, sunny winter day. *Maybe Olivia will want to get some lunch and go for a ride? Or not. She is still in heavy mourning over the loss of our Sandy Pines life and not thrilled about our new Maranatha life.* I could try a little bribery with a good lunch. Considering food is pretty sparse here, it's a win-win situation. Olivia agrees, and we set off for the hour drive and talk a little more about the college visits she's been on. She starts to open up a little bit more during our Panera stop.

It's still sunny as we near our turnoff for the cottage, but as always it's bitter cold along the lake. When we pull in the driveway we sit in the car and eyeball the snow-covered steps. All forty-seven of them are covered in ice and snow.

"Bundle up!" I say, zipping my neck into my coat as far as I can.

Olivia gives me a startled look. "Oh, you want me to get out?"

"Humor me," I say. "It's kind of a big moment. We're getting the keys!" We brave our way up the snowy steps, clinging to the railing like we are mountain-climbing instead of stair-climbing. We make it to the back door, and I have to remind her (and me) what we are walking into.

"It's not going to smell any better," I warn her. "If anything, it's worse!" I cover my nose with my hat as we enter. She agrees and we do a very quick walkthrough before heading back out into the fresh air. We really have nowhere else we want to go, so we head home and proceed with our regularly scheduled Sunday routine.

Sober Cycle

Olivia and I usually overtake the living room and catch up on the show we reserve to watch only together. No one else gets it, but we don't care. I unashamedly admit the show is CMT's *Dallas Cowboy Cheerleaders—Making the Team.* I pretend to be indulging her, but we both know that's not true. I'm just as caught up in it as she is. We pass the afternoon watching who will make the final cut, snoozing, and snacking for a few hours.

I love days like today. I'm surprised I don't feel worse. I marvel to myself quite a few times today. Later I'm awoken a few times from my Dallas Cowboy dreams by my angel friends texting me to see how I am doing.

Hey Sher, how are you doing today? Craig back yet???

No, he's not. I'm just hanging out with Olivia. It's a good day so far. ☺

Craig is expected home soon, and I'm not sure how I'm going to tell him what has transpired. I'm starting to regret the whole thing now and wish I hadn't been so theatrical. Olivia leaves for youth group around six p.m., and Craig still isn't home. I consider the hidden bottle—nearly full, I might add—and decide that it's OK to have a quick shot. I follow up with the obligatory tablespoon of peanut butter and handful of Doritos to mask vodka's possible lingering scent as I hear our garage door opening.

Craig walks in the door with the expectant, guarded look I've become accustomed to. Poor guy never knows what he could be walking into.

"How was your weekend?" he asks. He's studying my face so intently I feel like he can see right through me. He has always said that he can tell by my eyes if I'm drinking or not, so I'm careful not to look away when I reply.

164

"Oh, fine." I shrug. "Super quiet. I read and worked on a little project."

"Did you go out at all?" he asked.

"Nope, I was a hermit all weekend until—guess what!" Time for my hidden weapon of a planned subject-changer! I hold up the cottage key. "This happened!"

I fill him in on the condition of the cottage, and we go down the road of planning what we want to do. The distraction I planned is a total success! *I certainly don't want to ruin this very pleasant evening and drop the drinking bomb on him again. I'll tell him a different time.*

Craig goes off to shower and I have a little nip from my supply and make us food. I'm quite pleased with myself for the way I'm detoxing, appearing very efficient and with-it. Craig doesn't seem suspicious, and the rest of the night passes uneventfully while he does emails and I watch TV. We go to bed without any sort of conversation about drinking. Mission accomplished.

27

Revelation

Monday morning comes and I'm off to the pregnancy center. I'm feeling a bit more "off" than yesterday. The post-weekend chatter around the coffeepot is plentiful and also obstructing the coffee lane. As much as I don't want to engage in any of it, I have to if I want coffee, which I definitely do. I'm filling my travel mug for the third time before nine a.m. when the question comes. "Hey, Sherry, what'd you do this weekend?"

I'm not sweating over the question. I'm used to lying and easily deliver my usual Oscar-worthy performance. I know my lines. I've rehearsed. I'm well-prepared. "I did absolutely nothing. I had the house to myself and was incredibly lazy," I say, shutting my eyes a little to emphasize how dreamy it had been. I made staying home sound like the best thing ever and even got a few envious looks from a few coworkers.

I wonder what would happen if I would've slammed them with the truth? What if I had said, "Well, after Craig and Olivia left Friday night, I started drinking straight vodka. I slept-drank-repeated until I drank too much and freaked out that I had alcohol poisoning and was going to die. I called some friends who climbed in bed with me for the day, even though I was braless and smelled rancid. They stayed with me all day, and I promised them when they left that I was done drinking for good. However, surprise! I was lying. Then I went out and got more vodka and just drank less to be safe. Actually, I'm detoxing right now. That smell is alcohol coming out of my pores."

Probably wouldn't have gone over too well. I'll stick with the boring-weekend version.

As the day goes on, my detoxing tremors amp up and become harder to hide. When someone comes to stand by my desk, I quickly put my hands in my lap. *I need a drink.* To have any sort of conversation I have to concentrate hard before I respond. *What the heck happened to me over the weekend?*

Finally home and with a few minutes to myself, I try to drink but it's like my throat closes up and rejects the alcohol. I get nothing down. I try a few more times without any success. I'm getting really pissed off about this. I just want this anxiety to go away, I want relief, but it won't come.

One would think that at this moment I'd understand that quitting would be a great place to start. When your body is telling you not to drink and your mind is not wanting to listen, you have a powerful battle going on in your head. *Mental versus physical: Who will win? I'll get a last hurrah. I'll be the one to say when I'm done drinking.*

After a few more failed attempts I call it a night and go to bed fighting my craving. I wake up during the night a couple of times and, surprisingly, I don't feel anxious. But I do feel something else. I lay there quietly and know without a doubt that I'm feeling God's presence. His words to me are clear but firm. *This needs to be it. I'm giving you an open door. Walk away from alcohol and into my arms. I'm waiting.*

When I wake up in the morning, I feel the same calm. I wait patiently for Craig to leave so I can be alone with God. When Craig leans in for a kiss and the usual, "Have a great day, hon," I feel an urgency to tell him what I'm feeling. How I feel God is speaking into me to quit, but I want to explore this with him first.

I'm prompted to open the door to a conversation, so I grab Craig's hand when he starts to walk away. "Can we talk tonight?"

The fear on his face is evident as he replies. "No, I want to talk right now."

"No, not yet. Go to work and let's do the day the best we can and talk tonight, OK?"

Craig leaves me alone in the quiet, and I don't open my journal immediately. I just sit and wait with it on my lap, trying to quiet my mind and listen. The song "Revelation" by Third Day comes into my thoughts and I quickly google it. Music speaks to me like nothing else, and God knows that about me. I know this song is from him. So I pray. *Please, Lord, give me a revelation, I don't know what do. I am at a crossroads here and I know I need to choose.*

The tears run down my face and I am on my knees not recalling how I got there. My face is buried in my hands on the chair and I am sobbing into them. I feel my heart breaking into a million little pieces. The edges are jagged, and they're cutting me.

I know this is it: the point of no return. I need to be put back together. I'm so broken. I know I'm face to face with God and he's waiting for my answer. I feel grief. I lie down on the floor as I feel myself start to mourn what I'm saying goodbye to. *This shouldn't be so difficult!* I shouldn't love this thing, this substance that's almost destroyed me and everything I love. But I do. I cry out all these things to God: "Give me a revelation, Lord! Show me what to do!"

I don't know how long I lay there, but it was a while. I don't end the conversation while sobbing on the floor. I simply don't know what to say this time. God's heard it all before. So I just get up, walk into the kitchen, dig out the bottle from the back of the cupboard, and stare at it in my hands.

This liquid that remains has the power to take away everything, Sherry. Every single thing you love and every single thing you desire for your life. With one hand raised to God and the other unscrewing

168

the bottle over the sink, I say, "God, take it. I surrender my life with this demon and give it to you. I'm yours." The bottle is empty, but the smell of the vodka lingers and is putrid to my nostrils. I drop the bottle and now both hands are free, and now I'm raising both of them to God.

Bruised and beaten, I walk away from the war with alcohol I've been fighting for years. I don't feel any joy in this moment of what should be a victory. I feel like I've lost a war and am waving the white flag of surrender. Surrender means to give up—how is that a victory?

PART 10

EMPOWERED

28

Game On

Craig is home early. I knew he would be; he'd called a few times that day just to "see what I was up to." He doesn't do that unless he's worried that I'm drinking. I want to tell him I'm doing something productive on my day off, but the words "rigorous honesty" pop into my head every time the phone rings and I try to come up with an answer for him. Stupid AA and all their clichés have become ingrained in me somehow. *No more lies*, I think as I pick up the phone. My answer to him: "Not much."

When he calls for the third time, he's obviously decided to slaughter the elephant in the room. "Are you drinking?"

"No," I reply. "I'm not." I want to add, "Not today, not ever." I don't though. I've said this before, and my history of lying and drinking won't give him a reason to believe me this time either. "We'll talk tonight, OK?" I say softly.

"OK, as long as you're all right. I'll see you later."

I spend the day writing in my journal and talking to God about my upcoming conversation with Craig. I'm struggling with how to assure him that I'm done drinking. For good. In the past when I have declared this, I didn't focus much on being sober, much less sharing it with him. I'd bury it in grandiose plans of nutrition, fitness, and projects. Distractions are my specialty, and in the past I did just about everything but focus on the actual problem. Alcohol. Instead, I'd redirect my attention to everything else that I felt needed an overhaul. Always external, not internal.

Today the work is all internal. I finally come to the conclusion on this November day that I'll have to show my truth instead of trying to tell it. It won't be immediately apparent to Craig that I'm committed; of that I'm confident. *How can I assure him, Lord?*

I journal and write most of the afternoon. I write Craig a letter and plan to read it to him so I can keep my eyes on the paper instead of him. I don't want to watch the hurt and anger that I'm responsible for come over him once again. It feels like we're about to tune in to another rerun of a tiresome sitcom of our lives. I'm bolstered by this verse as I sit there, letter in hand:

> The LORD will fight for you; you need only to be still.
> (Exodus 14:14 NIV)

I'm still in the same chair when Craig comes in the door. I start to cry again. *Dang, how can I possibly have any more tears to cry?* But there they are, and they show no sign of stopping anytime soon.

"Hon?" His voice is laced with worry and concern as he kneels in front of me. Eye level. He takes my hands in his. "Talk to me." His caring tone, the love in his voice—I don't deserve this, but somehow I have it.

"I need to tell you what happened while you were gone. I wrote you a letter." I start to unfold it but he stops me.

"No, look at me. I don't want you to read me anything."

There goes an entire afternoon of effort. But I dive in and tell him everything. The plan, the scare, Robin coming over. Then running to the store for more and trying to drink and not being able to. I reveal much more than what I'd written in that letter. I tell him about my revelation this morning, and it sounds lame, almost manufactured. I don't know how to keep this from sounding like a predictable Christian novel. "Woman leads life of addiction and deceit, cries out to God, and is healed. The end."

For us, though, this is the beginning of a new novel. A true story about the shame of addiction and how hard the road to recovery is when temptation is everywhere. A story with chapters revealing a marriage based on honesty and navigating through the waters of sobriety together. *Does he feel this?* I think about what is ahead of us that has yet to be written. I'm scared to my core. I can't do this alone. I've asked God for help, and now I'm asking Craig.

Craig is quiet for a long time. His eyes are filled with tears that he makes no effort to hide. *Oh Lord, how I've hurt this man. I'm so sorry, so so sorry.* I look into his eyes, and through our tears we hold each other's hands and say nothing.

I have nothing left. Craig is not one to respond to anything quickly. He puts thought into every word he says, which most times I find maddening—but not now. This time would not be an exception, as it seems hours before he finally speaks. When he opens his mouth, my heart is pounding. I'd told God that I'd do whatever he asked, and I was terrified that Craig would lay down the R word. Rehab.

"You need help, to go to rehab."

And BOOM, there it is.

Craig goes on. "I cannot do this anymore. This is bigger than both of us. You know this and so do I."

I have no words (for once), so I just sit there and brace myself for more of what I don't want to hear but am going to anyway.

"You could've died!" And on these last words, his voice breaks and he turns away from me.

I take his face in my hands, turn it back toward me, and lock his eyes with mine. In a last-ditch effort to somehow get across to him that this time is different, I take a deep breath and dive in.

"Hon, you have no reason to believe me. I get it. Please hear me out though."

He nods slightly and waits for me to continue.

"I can't tell you how, what, or why, but I'm honestly positive I'll never drink again." I see the uncertainty flicker across his face, but I keep going. "Not just because I'm scared of the consequences. It's like I had a spiritual awakening or something. I can't explain it, but I know this is it. You have no reason to trust me; I get it. But I'm asking you to please believe me. Believe *in* me. I can do this, with you and with God."

He takes my hands from his, places them back in my lap, and stands up. "I need a minute," he says and walks into the kitchen.

I don't move. I'm frozen with fear, with the reality of what I'm seeing unfold. *Is he going to leave me? Send me to rehab? Lord, help us through this.* These are the only thoughts in my head, and I repeat them over and over until I work up the courage to join Craig in the kitchen. He's leaning over the counter on his elbows and doesn't face me when I put my hand gently on his back.

"I cannot do this ever again," he says quietly and turns to face me. "If you drink again, you will have two choices. The first will be to go to rehab to stay for thirty, sixty, ninety days—whatever it takes."

I'm trying to pay attention as my mind processes his words. *He said if. That means not this time—thank you, Jesus.*

Craig's words are slow and controlled as he continues. "The other choice is the one you make when you've chosen to drink and not go to rehab. Then you'll leave this house. I don't care where you go, but you are on your own."

My eyes tear up at the hard edge of hurt I hear in his words.

"I'll no longer protect our kids, our parents, or our friends from the truth that you're an alcoholic and have chosen this over them."

Game On

I say nothing. His words sound harsh, but I get it. I don't deserve another chance, but Craig's giving me one. I smile at him. "Game on."

He wraps his arms around me, and I feel safe. Loved.

"It's going to suck for a while," I say softly.

Pulling back so I can see his face, Craig replies, "Only if you let it."

29

The Rules of the Game

Consider it pure joy, my brothers and sisters, whenever you
face trials of many kinds.
—James 1:2 NIV

I read the verse and decide to add up the so-called joys I've
been through while being sober these past fifty days.

- A three-day power outage
- Hunting season—lots of alone time for me
- Thanksgiving, Christmas, and New Year's (and let's not
  forget New Year's Eve)
- Three family birthday celebrations
- Putting my phone through the washing machine
- An incident involving the garage door, my hatch, and
  Olivia

That's the short list, but in each item there are family
squabbles, escalated emotions, and things definitely not going
as planned—such as with power outages and putting your
phone on the spin cycle.

But I'm surviving. It feels a little surreal as I reflect early on
a Saturday morning. I've even been able to restart my attitude
when needed and not stay stuck in a pit when I fall in headfirst.

Take this morning. I was quietly heading into the bathroom while trying not to wake Craig when his arm shot out like a scene in a horror movie when the dead body moves and totally scares the crap out of you. When his hand grabbed my leg, causing me to scream (an obscenity), he muttered, "Take your pill" and rolled back over. I was furious. My good mood? Gone. *Geez, can I even pee before you say that?*

Craig means to take the Antabuse pill that he left on the bathroom counter for me. Part of our morning ritual is me swallowing this pill every single morning. He's not going so far as to watch me take it every single time, but he does ask if I have. Sometimes I'm extremely resentful of this pill. It tries to take the credit for my sobriety. While it's a tool I'm using, it's not flying solo here. This pill has no effect on me unless I drink, and the effect is horrible. I know this from experimentation in years past. My heart rate increases, and I turn bright red as I have a reaction to drinking that is truly terrifying and impossible to hide.

Take this morning, for instance. I'm up early just to seize the quiet. My time with God and my coffee has quickly become the best part of my day. The earlier I get up, the more time I have to dive into whatever it is God wants to speak into me.

I'm reading (more like studying) Rick Warren's *What on Earth Am I Hear For?*, a forty-day study taking me a lot longer than forty days to get through. There's just so much good stuff! It's speaking into me, cultivating a desire to find out my purpose. I feel like I've been fighting my way through life these past few years. I'm tired of fighting, and it feels good to let God take over. The day I surrendered my drinking I gave him the lead. Jesus take the wheel and all that. When I think back to my other sobriety runs, I can see and feel why this time is different.

I'm submissive, listening to whatever God tells me to do. So far he hasn't asked for anything other than my time and an intention to do better. There's a peace in me I haven't felt before. My impulses don't scare me (thanks to Antabuse). *Fine, the pill does get a lot of credit.* My impulses have gotten me into so much trouble in the past. I'd have the best of intentions for the day and one stray thought could lead me down the rabbit hole of drinking before I could gather my thoughts back for redirection.

I'd be cleaning my house and think, *Well, this would be more fun with a drink.* An hour later I'd be cleaning and drinking and then drink too much, quit cleaning, and pass out. Here's the thing: cleaning house is not supposed to be fun in the first place. My thought is, instead of drinking to get through the mundaneness of cleaning, we should just hire a cleaning lady. Problem solved! Maybe eventually, but for now when I have a thought like that, I can quickly shut it down because it's not a possibility. So yes, it does give me some insurance and—more importantly—it's getting me over the hump as I make new habits that don't have anything to do with drinking.

I'm better than before I got sober every day. Even when I don't do life well, it's still better to be a sober jerk than a drunk jerk.

All these things I'm doing take place when I'm alone. That's where life is easiest. It's when I'm not alone that things aren't so smooth.

Craig and I are running into some friction. The honeymoon phase of support for the sober life has passed. The first month we went to at least fifteen movies. He would walk in the door and ask for my number. It started out as a joke, because it isn't a secret that I can go from 0 to 10 rather quickly. The number 0 would mean that I'm crawling out of my skin and want to kill everyone. A 10 would be that I'm June Cleaver and here's your slippers. Anything under a 5 would mean that we walk right back out the door and go to the movies to kill a few hours. No talking. Just a small fortune in popcorn and sugar, but it worked for a while. Then I could go to bed when we got home and start over again in the morning.

Now we're at odds about a few things, the big one being sex. I don't want to go into a lot of detail here, but there are two things I've determined are easier with liquid courage: dancing and sex. Not together mind you, but in my experience these are both actions you do best by losing any inhibitions. This bodes well after a glass of wine (or three).

Not so much with sobriety. Craig and I had to learn a lot of things over, starting from scratch—and it's not always easy. We were at a wedding recently, and I ran out onto the dance floor with my friends and suddenly, something felt off. I'm dancing like Steve Martin in *The Jerk*. Where is my rhythm? Did I ever have any? Probably not, but I didn't care because I was drinking, and I wasn't the least bit concerned about my moves or who was watching. I could snap my fingers in eighties delight and not care in the least that my Spanx were slipping with every twist. I could sing at the top of my lungs and not care who heard me.

Those days are gone. At least for now. Maybe it'll get better someday, but I'm not that concerned. It's not like I'm dancing every day. Besides, there's always YouTube if I need to learn some moves.

I think we tend to glamorize life a little when we can't do something. My favorite analogy on this comes from one time when a friend had a broken leg and said to her husband, "I can't wait to run when this cast is off."

He looked at her and said, "You didn't run before you had the cast on."

She probably wanted to kill him, but he made a good point.

Which brings me back to the second thing that's easier and more enjoyable when inhibitions are surrendered: sex. Just like a broken leg, intimacy issues have to heal before you can walk. You want to run? That'll require training and won't feel natural for a long time. You'll need to take it slow and not have high expectations about what it's going to be like when you reach the finish line. You may never go back to the way it was before you broke your leg. Then again, you might be even better than before you broke your leg!

Quit making up scenarios in your mind about how great your leg was before you broke it. Your spouse needs to be patient while you heal, and with patience and understanding, you'll catch up. Our sex life needs time to heal. Right now it might be best if I put myself in a body cast, taking away the sex option completely. If that were true, we'd be forced to address the emotional side of our sober sex life and could take baby steps in the right direction when the cast came off.

But it *is* getting better, easier, every day. Overall I'm finding out how to live without alcohol. I don't miss the inner turmoil that controlled my thoughts when I lived a secret life of addiction. *Will I? Shall I? When can I? Do others know?* All that's gone, and I'm finding that it's opened up a lot of useful space in my brain. This newfound peace of mind is a good place to stay and rest for a while.

30

The Taste of Victory

The harder the conflict, the more glorious the triumph.
—Thomas Paine

The Ride4Life 2014 is happening on the tail end of my first year of sobriety. I'm pedaling in a different direction. Still to cross a finish line, but this finish line won't bring me back to a life of drinking. My thoughts are not constantly invaded with the dilemma of whether or not I'll drink when I get home. As I approach my one-year sober anniversary, I'm confident that I won't. It's surreal that I've gone almost a year without a drop of alcohol. The below verse has been swirling around in my head, so last night I looked it up and decided to make it my focus while I ride today.

> Be alert, be present. I'm about to do something brand-new.
> It's bursting out! Don't you see it? (Isaiah 43:19)

I've learned to navigate sober through cocktail hours, weddings, graduations, family trips, business trips, girls' nights, and holidays by doing life one day at a time and staying close to God. While that is the short list of accomplishments, I'm proud of checking each "first" off the list of sober successes.

I'm feeling other thoughts swirling around, and I'm quiet on the ride this morning as I try to make sense of them.

I'm doing this Ride4Life for the purpose that it was created: to raise funds and awareness for the ministry I work for. In years past I wanted this ride to get me sober and then keep me sober. I thought doing it might earn respect from my friends and family whom I had let down so many times. I've been working on relationships this past year, and many have been beautifully restored. There's still a lot of work to be done when I get off this bike. I have to continue owning up to my mistakes to many of my friends and being open to making some new friends along the way.

I'm pondering this as we ride along the lakeshore on this second to the last day of my fifth Ride4Life. It's a gorgeous Indian summer day, and I am hearing murmurings from my teammates of a Lake Michigan plunge at the end of today's ride. Our route takes us to a quiet road, weaving us around an inland lake. We embrace the opportunity to relax and ride in pairs and be in conversation.

I'm last in the ride formation, and I watch this unfold in front of me and am grateful to see my dear friend Bonnie hang back to ride with me. Maybe it's the beauty of the moment in the sparkling lake, the warmth of the sun, and affection for my teammates that brings me to fresh tears.

This is a reoccurring event in my newfound sober life. I've become an emotional train wreck. Tears can appear for seemingly no reason whatsoever! A child in the grocery store who smiles at me can bring me into a full-on bawl in seconds. Olivia texting me good night from her dorm room can generate enough tears to soak my pillow. I'm absolutely helpless over this and have been learning to just let them flow. Feels cleansing.

"So why right now?" Bonnie notices my tears and asks the question even though she's accustomed to my unannounced tearful moments. "What's wrong? Did something happen?"

"Not really." I shrug.

She nods and encourages me to unpack what's stirring me to tears.

"I'm thinking about tomorrow, when we ride in and cross the finish line."

"Go on."

"So, I don't even know if they are coming. My kids, I mean. They haven't paid much attention to details this past year about the ride. Old news, I guess."

Bonnie nods. "Maybe so, but I get you wanting them to be there. I hope my kids are there with the grandbabies!"

"I don't know. I want something more. I don't know how to explain it." We let the conversation die off and ride in silence together.

I continue thinking this over. *I know what I want, but do I have a right to it? Do I deserve anything at all? I just want them to want me. To seek me out and take pride in me.* That's supposed to be my job. Moms praise kids, not the other way around. But I want it anyway. Then it hits me.

I want the Rockford Game.

I had one takeaway from my brief outpatient stint a few years ago, a takeaway that I use often in life and especially on these rides when I need to dig deep to keep myself propelling forward. In IOP (Intensive Outpatient treatment) I'd had an assignment to think about a happy, significant moment in life that I treasure. To write the event in detail and imbed it on my heart to pull out when I needed a joy moment. I wrote about the Rockford Game.

ഓഓഓ

My son played high school football, and if I had to pick a highlight of his teenage years, this memory would be my choice. I was not exactly a football fan before my son was on the field. Growing up, my dad and I had this game where I would curl my fingers into a fist and he would cup them with his big hand and press on my fingers until I said, "I love football!" My Dad loved to ask me, "Now that Loren plays, do you like football?" To which I would reply yes even though my dad still might inflict a little hand torture anyway.

Loren was a scrawny, fast, and little quarterback while growing up. Going into high school, the quarterback competition was stiff and he had backed off from playing high school football.

In Loren's sophomore year we were in the stands with our usual bunch of football friends. I noticed Loren scanning the stands, looking for us. He spotted us, waved, and started making his way up through the crowd.

"Money," I said to Craig. That's usually why the kids came looking for us. But this time I was wrong. When Loren finally got to us, he said with a big smile, "I'm going to play next year!"

"That's great!" we said. That's what you do as parents, right? Encourage your kids? Loren walked away beaming over his announcement—and carrying five bucks.

"Not sure what that looks like for him," Craig said. "He's kind of in between on the growth chart. I'm not sure he'll get any playing time."

We shouldn't have doubted our son's drive to get what he wanted. Instead of concentrating on getting faster, he hit the weight room. By his junior year he had doubled in size—literally. He was getting a little playing time, sometimes alongside his best friend. He continued to work hard toward his goal of cracking the starting lineup.

That night was the game against our biggest rival, Rockford, the crème de la crème of all small-town football rival games. If Hudsonville beat Rockford, we'd be unstoppable and on our way to defeating every other team as well as on a direct path to the state championship.

Loren and his buddies had a game-day routine. They would head straight to Subway after school for a foot-and-a-half-long sub. It was a ritual they followed to the letter. I tiptoed around the house as Loren went downstairs after the Subway ritual to get ready. I had made sure his uniform was spotless and ready for play. I, too, was caught up in the fever of football, and I left early to get in line for good seats with a few of my friends.

The game was a nail-biter, but the victory was sweet! The final score: 7-6 Hudsonville! When the clock ran out, the crowd went wild. We scrambled to rush the field and congratulate our boys. The band was playing the victory song, and the cheerleaders threw each other high in the air, and the players? They were body-slamming and back-slapping in the euphoria that comes with a hard-won victory.

Craig and I paused at the top of the steps leading down to the field to look for our son. I scanned the crowd for my number 56, and when I spotted him, I could see he was looking for someone too. I smiled to myself, as I was sure he was looking for his girlfriend, Stephanie, and not his mother. We started making our way to him through the thick crowd.

I'll never forget the moment his eyes found mine and he yelled, "Mom!" Loren broke through the crowd that separated us, picked me up, and gave me the tightest hug I'll ever remember from him.

"Mom, Mom, we did it. They said we couldn't, but we did."

We were crying happy tears. I looked over his shoulder and saw Craig's eyes filling as well. I felt victory in that moment. Victory as the mom of this boy who would never be able to grasp what that moment meant to me.

There are many moments in life where the title of *Mom* is honored—Happy Mother's Day, Happy Birthday Mom, Mother of the Bride. But those are planned and expected. This was a spontaneous accolade, and I felt so loved and valued. Granted, I was set down quickly so he could hug his dad too. I stood quietly behind them savoring the moment. I wanted to treasure it forever, and when assigned to write about a moment such as this, I could recall it vividly.

Sober Cycle

That's what I want to feel if they are all there at the end of the ride tomorrow. Sherry, stay peaceful. I am loved and valued by my Heavenly Father. That needs to be enough.

> Now to him who is able to do immeasurably more than all we ask or imagine, according to his power that is at work within us. (Ephesians 3:20 NIV)

I was about to find out what "immeasurably more" would mean in my life. I was about to ride across the finish line for the Ride4Life and straight into the start of something so beautiful it is truly more than I could ask or imagine.

As the sun sets this evening, thirteen people in bike jerseys hold hands and run into Lake Michigan. It's a moment of unity on the ride, and I'll savor that moment and write about it later—just like the Rockford Game.

ℰℰℰ

I can hear the cheers and whistles of the gathered crowd as we ride across the same bridge we'd crossed just a week ago. I spot my husband first, and the threatening tears (of course) begin to fall down my face. His facial expression shows love and pride for me. As I ride past him, leading twelve riders to the finish, he mouths "I love you" and winks at me. Then I'm in the parking lot and surrounded by *my whole family*! All of them! Abby, Joe, Loren, Stephanie, Olivia, Craig, and even my mom. I'm reduced to speechlessness amid their hugs and unable to do anything but cry happy tears of gratitude that this bunch of Hoppens love me this much and that they are mine to love back—all mine.

After things settle down, we head inside for food and fellowship. I hold hands tightly with Craig as we are led in prayer. Olivia has to leave for a wedding, so I give her a hug goodbye much earlier than I want to, but life goes on. It's not

188

all about the Ride4Life anymore. Loren and Stephanie seem a little antsy to get going too. *Oh well, I'm still glad they all came.*

"Hey Mom," said Loren. "Walk out with us. We have a little something for you."

"OK," I said, turning to Abby and Joe. "I'll be right back."

Abby started to stand up. "We're going to get going too."

On our way out I caught Abby's eye and whispered, "Do you know what this is about?"

She shook her head. "I know nothing."

We gathered around Loren's truck and he reached inside and handed me a gift bag. "This is for you, Mom. We just wanted to get you a little something to show you how proud we are of you."

"Is this from all of you?"

Loren grinned. "Nope, just Steph and me."

I reached my hand into the bag, came in contact with something soft, and immediately knew what it was. I started crying before I even pulled it out of the bag, confusing everyone else until I showed them what had triggered the latest waterworks.

"I'm going to be Grandma, and you're going to be Grandpa, Mr. Hoppen!" Our family erupted into cheers, and I gave Loren a hug, whispering, "Thank you. No greater gift," into his ear. I have my Rockford Game.

Epilogue

Craig and I sit across from each other in my home office. Me, in my white-and-gold brass-trimmed desk chair and he perched awkwardly on a dainty, green velvet "lady's" chair. I've asked him to read chapter 28, "Game On," for accuracy and to see if he has anything to add. Instead, he has asked me to read it out loud.

I keep breaking down, barely able to get through. Reading it out loud to Craig has brought on an onslaught of raw emotion as we relive those last painful days of my drinking career. I finish reading, set my laptop down, and reach for my husband. Together, we dissolve into tears and mourn all of the darkness of addiction we've been through together.

Craig is wiping his eyes. "That was hard to hear."

I nod. "It was much more painful to speak it than to type it. I would much rather write about the last six years of sober life than my drinking years."

"You're telling the real story. How much it hurts, how it destroys everyone it touches, and how hard it is to get out of. That will help people a lot more than if you started with a happy ending."

"True," I say. "But I'm still so sorry for everyone that I hurt along the way. And even though I don't carry that pain daily anymore, it will always bother me. I have to ask for grace in this journey every single day."

> Because of the extravagance of those revelations, and so I wouldn't get a big head, I was given the gift of a handicap to keep me in constant touch with my limitations. Satan's

angel did his best to get me down; what he in fact did was push me to my knees. No danger then of walking around high and mighty! At first I didn't think of it as a gift, and begged God to remove it. Three times I did that, and then he told me,

My grace is enough; it's all you need.
My strength comes into its own in your weakness.

Once I heard that, I was glad to let it happen. I quit focusing on the handicap and began appreciating the gift. It was a case of Christ's strength moving in on my weakness. Now I take limitations in stride, and with good cheer, these limitations that cut me down to size—abuse, accidents, opposition, bad breaks. I just let Christ take over! And so the weaker I get, the stronger I become. (2 Corinthians 12:7–10)

୫୦୫୦୫୦

I started writing this book for anyone who is struggling with addiction, but it ended up bringing me healing and closure as well. If there is any takeaway in my story, it's that you aren't alone. In going back through my journals of the past ten years, I've learned so much about myself and what I did to get to this place of redemption. Redemption means "deliverance" or "rescue."

I used to say "restoration," but I know now that is an inaccurate description of my journey through addiction. To be restored would mean that I was brought back to who I used to be, which is simply not true. I'm not her.

I often say I don't like to think about the woman I would be had I not chosen this path of alcoholism. I'd still be trying to deal with the hard knocks of life in my own strength. Life would be about things and what I could have and achieve, again in my own will. I would not have learned what it truly means to "give it to God." I would not know the true meaning of "until death do us part" and found the love of my life for the second time.

I quit focusing on the handicap and began appreciating the gift.

Addiction hardens your heart. You become a person with a hard outer shell that nothing can penetrate. You internalize nothing because you have this numbing substance protecting you from feeling anything hurtful or joyous. You're deadened to every emotion. No matter how hard you try, there's one voice you can't block, for he is persistent.

That one is God and only God. God's love scares you. You know what he wants from you and yet you cannot fathom it. You just don't know how to do life without your drug of choice. In the pit of my addiction there were many times I felt like Jonah, rotting in the belly of a whale because I kept running from what God was asking me to do.

November 6, 2013, when I was on my knees in surrender, I was desperate to be done fighting the alcohol, my family, myself, and most of all God. Surely if I could fight this hard to stay an alcoholic, I could fight just as hard to stay sober. The grace that God continued to show me each and every day, even while I was drinking, is the only thing that saved me from complete self-destruction and saved my life.

However, it was up to me to give up my endless search for a way out when the answer had been right in front of me the whole time. I had to trust him with all of my heart and be willing that I would do whatever he asks of me. When I did, the miracle of a brand-new life became possible.

When you're in the throes of addiction, in my case alcoholism, you cannot see a way out. It's virtually impossible to wrap your mind around doing life sober. Trust me when I say, "He will make a way."

Addiction looks like many things. A drug, a drink, a habit, an activity—the list is endless. Whatever that is for you, it's time to leave it behind and start living. Really living. I promise you this: *you will be amazed*. Life will never be the same.

Epilogue

Blessings and Peace,
Sherry

> And now, isn't it wonderful all the ways in which this distress has goaded you closer to God? You're more alive, more concerned, more sensitive, more reverent, more human, more passionate, more responsible. Looked at from any angle, you've come out of this with purity of heart. (2 Corinthians 7:11)

If you enjoyed this book, will you consider sharing the message with others?

Let us know your thoughts at info@ironstreammedia.com. You can also let the author know by visiting or sharing a photo of the cover on our social media pages or leaving a review at a retailer's site. All of it helps us get the message out! Facebook.com/IronStreamMedia

———————

Iron Herring, Ascender Books, New Hope® Publishers, Iron Stream Books, and New Hope Kidz are imprints of Iron Stream Media, which derives its name from Proverbs 27:17, "As iron sharpens iron, so one person sharpens another."

This sharpening describes the process of discipleship, one to another. With this in mind, Iron Stream Media provides a variety of solutions for churches, ministry leaders, and nonprofits ranging from in-depth Bible study curriculum and Christian book publishing to custom publishing and consultative services. Through our popular Life Bible Study, Student Life Bible Study brands, and New Hope imprints, ISM provides web-based full-year and short-term Bible study teaching plans as well as printed devotionals, Bibles, and discipleship curriculum.

For more information on ISM and its imprints, please visit IronStreamMedia.com